重新定义

REDEFINITIONS

“70后”艺术中的质疑精神

THE QUESTIONING SPIRIT OF SEVENTIES GENERATION ART

主编/杭春晓

Let's IF 如果 ART

天津人民美術出版社

Tianjin People's Fine Arts Publishing House

目录

Catalog

"70后"的人生，在不确定性的世界中，寻找观看世界时确定的通道。

The 70s generation, finding itself in an indefinite world, is searching for a path toward a definite vision of the world.

杭春晓

Hang Chunxiao

王　屹

Wang Yi

1971年出生于北京，网络媒体人。1999年加入新浪网，现任新浪尚品/收藏频道总监。

Wang Yi , born in Beijing China, Internet media figure, joined Sina.com in 1999, is curently director of Editorial Dept. - Style/Collection Channel .

不确定性

——“70后”存在经验的自我检讨

杭春晓 | 王 屹

杭春晓／ 概括“70后”艺术的时候，多流行“青春残酷”或“卡漫”之类的阐释。但在我看来，这种阐释过于简单，或者说并不贴切。尤其是“青春残酷”，隐含了一个相当荒谬的前提：只有经历剧烈的社会动荡，人才能拥有深刻的社会认知，否则只会进入自身世界的局部体验中。也许，“70后”艺术家缺乏前辈人激烈的人生冲撞，但在他们看似平淡的生活中，生存际遇的不确定，却也给他们提供了理性审视生活的机会，并让他们以一种怀疑色彩的眼光反思生活中既定的价值判断，而非什么“浅层伤害”带来的“自我迷恋”。从某种意义上说，“70后”的人生，是在不确定性的世界中，寻找观看世界时确定的通道。这个展览，正是试图从一批不同类型的，具有代表性的“70后”艺术家的创作中，探讨并显现这种不同于上一代艺术的特质。

历史记忆

这一代人，确实存在着某种生存体验的共性，应该说，这与整个大的时代状态有关。比如说，尤其是上世纪70年代早期出生的人，对70年代重大历史事件是具有记忆的,并且这种记忆不同于上一代人。比如领袖的逝世、“四人帮”的倒台，以及“十一届三中全会”的召开等等，在当时留给他们的记忆就是一种符号化的，但却是直接的感知。80年代开始，他们进入自己的少年、青年期，改革开放带来了大量新奇的文化形式，加之当时还未能够彻底消化的各种新奇思想，呈现为多元碰撞的成长环境。在这样的环境中，他们的人生时常处于某种价值判断的不稳定状态中。90年代以后，经济大潮迅猛冲击，又再次抹平了他们曾经的体验、记忆，而替以新的庸俗化的现实性。从某种意义上说，他们面对自己的生活，并没有多少可以自己选择的机会，就像是被潮水冲着走，没有太多的主动性，有的更多的是不断调整自己的生存姿态。 ／王 屹

杭春晓／ 是啊，生活对我们而言，更多的是被动接受的权力，而非主动选择的权力。并且，这种不确定的状态中，我们还试图找到确定的方式去面对。或许，这就是你所说的，调整自己生存姿态的那种东西。

这里有一种悖论，就是我们在不确定性中试图寻找确定的东西。在我看来，这和“70后”的教育仍然延续了宏大叙事性的思想有关，从某种角度上看，他们最初的思想资源，恰恰还是从黑格尔到马克思的唯物辩证法。 ／王 屹

杭春晓／ 而且，这种东西还是已经被中国改造过的东西，并非原装货（笑）。其实，在后来的阶段中，对于这种东西的反思，并试图通过其他思想资源加以改造，这个过程是很漫长的。

没有一个长时间的过程，不容易改变的，那种教育是伴随着每一次升学考试的权力规定，而不断强化的东西。其实，重新想想，那种教育带来的影响是很顽固的。 ／王 屹

杭春晓／ 呵呵，无论我们现在怎样试图重构，有时候还会不时流露出那种东西的影响。比如说宏大叙事的历史观，我们现在试图阐释“70后”艺术的行为，是不是就掉入到这种思想的陷阱中了？

也许。但换一个角度来看，我们还是可以从我们的生存细节中获知某种感觉的。 ／王 屹

杭春晓／ 这一点，我是坚信的。比如初中毕业的时候，老师会鼓励你考中专。这种鼓励行为的背后，其实暗含了一种权力化的规定——那就是中专毕业后，分配工作，直接就成为国家干部。要知道，成为国家干部，在社会主义中国的概念中，那是被描绘出的某种理想人生。于是，我们有些同学接受了这个观念。结果，现在回头来看他们的生活，你就会发现命运和他们开了一个大大的玩笑。那么，在这个玩笑的背后，恰是一种看似确定的生存价值，就在我们的眼前，以直接可感的方式崩溃了。

是啊，我们在成长的每一个节点，总会有些人告诉你该怎么做，在当时看来确实应该这样。但过不了两年的时间，你就又会重新发现，那时的选择是多么的荒谬。这种经验，在“70后”的成长中，毫无疑问，是具有普遍性的。而我们的青春期，在经历多次这样的变化之后，某种不信任、怀疑的内在意识，就会自然而然地产生，而并非是通过理性反思之后才获得的。 ／王 屹

杭春晓／ 确实，“70后”的成长经验中，怀疑主义是天然的情绪。

比如说1976年，毛泽东去世。那时，我们家还因为成分问题在农村下放。在我的记忆中，那时候的大队，就是一个灵堂。到处都是黑色的条幅，写着“沉痛悼念伟大领袖”，到处都是白色的花圈和挽幛。村里的大喇叭一直播着哀乐，还有广播里念的悼词，不断重复播放，讲述毛泽东的历史。大家都被组织在一起，也都是非常沉痛的状态，而且这种状态一定也是非常真诚的。但在我的记忆中，这一切却因为一件小事而变得极富戏剧性色彩——因为大队文书忙着写挽联，旁边有个人伸着脸看他，文书就用毛笔在那个人脸上刷了一下，成为花脸，两个人一下就热闹了起来。于是，就在那一刻，所有的人都笑了起来，仿佛沉痛的东西，突然被滑稽的东西就取代了。这件事，在我的记忆中，印象特别深，因为刚刚还是如此悲哀的状态，一下子就可以变得极为滑稽。 ／王 屹

杭春晓／ 也许当时，你并不能了解这种转变意味着什么。但伴随着成长，这种东西会重新出现在记忆中，并且被重新描绘，重新理解。

对，这种东西在我们的记忆中是非常多的。比如说，70年代末80年代初的时候，我住在北京的一个胡同。有一天，刚从护城河捞完鱼回来，就发现胡同里一个人都没有，原来电视上在播放刘少奇的追悼会。其实，那时候的追悼会很多，而且一碰到这种追悼会，街上都很少有人，大多一个院子里围满了人，一起看着一台电视里的追悼会。而且，大人就会给你解释，说什么这是怎么回事，当初又怎么怎么了的。 ／王 屹

杭春晓／ 那种感觉，就是一种颠覆感，感觉什么东西都可以反过来重新说。

/王　屹

是啊，什么东西都和当初不一样，都可以反过来。而且，还都充满了权威感，无论是否定一个事情，还是重新肯定一个事情，都充满了权威。那么，这种记忆积累的结果，就是我们会逐渐认为，一件事情颠过来又颠过去，是非常正常的。

杭春晓／

我小时候，生活在一个相对偏远的矿山，也有着类似的记忆。比如说，我一边在学校的某个拐角看到“打倒叛徒某某”，然后一边又被教育，他被平反了。其实，这种东西在当时可能并不能理解，甚至也不当回事。但在自己成长的过程中，不断遇到类似的事情时，这种记忆就会成为一种思想资源，会不断浮现出来影响你的判断，直至最后，你会确信，这个世界很少有一个东西可以让你确信。

/王　屹

这听上去，多少有点像悖论，但却是事实。比如说，我在幼儿园的时候学儿歌，学的是“古代有个投降派，名叫宋江把人害，如今有个保皇派……”，后来，大家又一起念诗怀念周总理。很快，“四人帮”倒台了，幼儿园里竖起四个人的头像，让小孩拿沙包砸。你说孩子能懂什么？一会儿这样，一会那样。也许当时，只是让你觉得好玩，但在今后的成长过程中，它们却都是让你怀疑一切确定性的重要源头。因为那种悖论感，太直接了。

生存体验

杭春晓／

1990年播放的《渴望》，应该是“70后”生活的一个转折点。从那以后，政治话题对我们的直接影响开始消退，一切的生活目标，一下子转向了“好人一生平安”的旋律中。于是，“70后”的青春，从80年代懵懵懂懂的理想主义，转向了此后的物质主义、功利主义。

/王　屹

那种转变，其实也不是我们自主选择的，而是社会整体转向的力量，甚至还包括了流行文化崛起之类的因素。

杭春晓／

确实，在当时的记忆中，好像港台文化都是时尚的、先进的。比如说小虎队，当他们重新出现在前两年春晚的舞台上，我都诧异，当年怎么就会那么喜欢。这种喜欢，恐怕不仅是因为年少的原因，可能与整个社会转型中的虚无感有关。好像突然间，人们就是需要这种简单、直接，甚至肤浅的东西。

/王　屹

从流行文化来说，还是要从邓丽君开始。刚开始的时候，都是从那时并不合法的短波收音机中听到的，那种音乐和当时能够听到的或民族化或革命化的东西都不一样，是一种个体化的感受，而不是集体主义的东西。

杭春晓／

这种东西，对试图走出集体主义限定的每一个人，都是具有启蒙性的。

/王　屹

当时或许没有这种明确的意识，但它恰到好处地表达了某种青春期的朦胧感，而这种东西和我们受到的灌输，是完全不一样的。所以，它就特别有吸引力。后来，又跟着比我们年龄大一些的人听崔健的《一无所有》，也许我们不能像他们一样理解这首歌背后的东西，但那种扯着嗓子，发泄一种不知道从哪里来的情绪，却是特别棒的感觉。

杭春晓／ 这种感觉，也许到今天，还是一种游离的、不可确定的情绪。但它绝非完全个人化的东西，还是和那个时代的社会体验发生关联。

／王 屹 当然。现在分析那首歌，我们可以说，那种感觉是一个社会转变期中的精神虚无状态。比如说，那时候的人们，无论是就业，还是知识储备，都无甚可言。但却又要在这个时期脱离曾经的集体主义，走向独立生存的阶段。于是，一种毫无准备的慌乱感，自然会产生类似《一无所有》中呐喊般的情绪。虽然，这种东西对"70后"的人来说，未必那么明确，但他们的青春无疑和这种情绪有关。

杭春晓／ 不同于上一代人的清晰反叛，"70后"的反叛与呐喊，往往是在时代转变的牵引下发生，却又并不那么具有目标。于是，"70后"就是在这种不具明确指向的呐喊中，开始了自己对于生活的思考。

／王 屹 这是一个有意思的呐喊。

杭春晓／ 对。因为呐喊的目标并不那么清晰，所以"70后"往往会在成长的过程中，轻视一种具体明确的结果，而更倾向于审视这种结果产生的过程。

／王 屹 没有办法不这样。因为，我们的成长经历中，充满了这种结果的不断被颠覆，我们不得不形成一种对于这种确定性结果的不信任。

杭春晓／ 不信任，正是源于不断的被否定。

／王 屹 当时的家长、老师，对于学生过早张扬自己的个性，都秉持着否定的态度。他们的教育，还是试图用一种集体化的理想模式塑造孩子。但我们这些孩子的生存现实，却又不能提供这种集体主义的环境，因为所有人都不断地被这个时代抛离出既定轨道。这种成长经验中，充满了悖论。我还记得，那时候，曾经热议过一个事件，就是一个大学生为救一个掏粪工而死了，到底值不值。这件事，我记得初一的政治课上有辩论会，正方认为人的价值是平等的，反方认为他们的社会价值是不等的。

杭春晓／ 其实，这样的讨论，现在看来，结果并不重要。重要的是，我们为何那样判断。

／王 屹 确实，但类似的讨论却给"70后"的人带来一种困惑——生活似乎并不存在着我们在教育中所接受到的确定答案。从某种意义上看，"70后"的成长经历，一方面是个体开始从家庭走出，试图在社会寻找精神资源，但同时却是中国社会确定性精神资源相对虚无的时期。那个时候的整个社会，也像"70后"的青春期一样，自己也正处于稳定性精神资源的"断奶期"。

杭春晓／ 身处这样的“断奶期”，我们对于社会的精神求助，就会显得回馈无力。甚至，在你不断从身边寻找思想资源的同时，你会发现，那些所谓的思想资源，都是那么的不确定，处于一种动荡之中。前面刚刚告诉你的东西，后面就会否定掉。于是，你也会跟着再一次否定，就感觉自己是被甩来甩去的状态。

你对世界的判断，也因此而不断调整。 ／王 屹

杭春晓／ 很多时候想起来，我们会觉得自己的成长经验中，有着太多不靠谱、不确定的东西。往往当你习惯一种认知的时候，事实就会告诉你，那种认知相当不靠谱。比如，我记得小时候看《地道战》之类的片子，就会非常感慨，我们生活在幸福之中，但这个世界上还有很多人是生活在“白色恐怖”中，生活在水生火热中。但，随后的生存经验告诉你，那种想法极其荒唐。于是，你便会天然对于那种权力化的告诫，保持警惕。

对于集体主义的规定化，也是如此。 ／王 屹

杭春晓／ 是的。我小时候生活在一个矿山中，是那种典型的社会主义工业聚落形态。一切的生活依靠，都来源于矿山的集体。我对那种东西，可以说是建立了一种依赖感的信任，觉得只要在这个集体中，就有着一种安全。但后来，父母相继下岗，甚至两三年里拿不到工资。你想，这种生活的无所适从，一下子让那个曾经看似安全的体制，变得极不安全。就在那个时候，我从媒体上读到的东西，却和现实生活的感觉完全相背。那么，自然地，你便会对这种集体化的东西，产生某种怀疑。并因此，对一切具有权力界定、描述的东西，保持一种警惕。

阅读经验

“70后”的这种带有不信任感的生存体验，使得生活的影像对我们而言，时常处于一种飘渺不定的感觉中，就像《浮士德》里的一句诗：我眼前的所有已遥遥隐退，渺茫的往事却一一现形。 ／王 屹

杭春晓／ 这种感觉，也有点像武侠小说。那时候，读这种东西都不能光明正大，总是偷偷摸摸的。其实，现在想起来，大人们确实不够淡定。孩子看点这种东西，无非是一种幻想体验的满足。但那时候，这种书在家长、老师眼里，却是和某种社会不良习性有关联，总是一味地打压，认为这种阅读行为就是不学好。但，压制不仅没能控制局面，往往还适得其反，让我们越发迷恋小说里那种不真实的想象。

“70后”的阅读经验，似乎不成系统。从皮皮鲁到金庸，从琼瑶阿姨到王朔，从高加林到王小波，从朦胧诗到聂鲁达，从社会主义到萨特，一切的东西，都是在变荡中成为阅读文本的。而且，往往是很多的阅读碎片，伴随着人的成长，在不停消化、整合。 ／王 屹

杭春晓／ 也可以这么说，在“70后”的阅读中，缺乏权威的东西。尤其是在他们的青年期，很少能够有某种东西，能真正构建一种思考方式。我身边很多的朋友，其实大多是在青春期之后，才慢慢消化掉各种阅读，形成自己审视的立场、态度。呵呵，他们大多都是晚熟品种。

这种晚熟而杂食的阅读体验，从某种角度上看，也正是整个转型期社会，思想内核不稳定的显现。／王　屹

杭春晓／ 但这种理性判断，在最初的阅读中，是无法清晰的。但总是有那么一种感觉，认为文本中的某种东西不靠谱。比如当时读路遥《平凡的世界》，虽然也很享受那种并不真实的个人奋斗，但对书里描述的东西，却总将信将疑。最突出的就是关于田晓霞的死，我就觉得她一定要死，否则她的父亲，就不真实得有些离谱了。为什么呢？因为我就一直不相信，一个省委书记会支持自己的女儿和孙少平这样的工人谈恋爱。当然，也许在比我们大一些的人中，这种怀疑是不需要的。

但是，你一边怀疑这种东西，一边又非常享受这种东西。／王　屹

杭春晓／ 是的。

其实，“70后”阅读中的混杂，也使得他们无法回避各种东西的混杂性影响。比如说，现在的“70后”，在趋于理性主义的成熟中，却难免不会流露出某种与此相悖的抒情主义、英雄主义的东西。或许，一种个体与集体的悖论，就是在一直影响着“70后”群体。／王　屹

杭春晓／ 这还突出表现为对宏大叙事立场的暧昧姿态。一方面，他们试图摆脱这种思维方式，保持对于这种方式背后各种权力意识的警惕，但同时却又时常会以这种方式来思考问题。

比如说，我们今天的对话，试图对“70后”进行定义，是否也是这种思考方式的流露呢？／王　屹

杭春晓／ 没错，就是有这种嫌疑。但是，我们往往会说，我们所进行的判断，并非一种价值化的判断，不是一种逻辑化的定义，而是一种经验的描述，正如我们现在试图对于我们自身的生存经历进行一种描述，而非判断。

也许是这样。但“70后”时常会在这种立场中背离自己的初衷，因为在我们的生存体验中，依然会有意识、无意识地感受到这种思维模式。甚至，只要这种模式存在，我们还会不自觉地为这种模式添砖加瓦。“70后”的人，依然还是希望从自身的精神资源中，寻找到能够搭建这种模式的东西。诸如说，思考人活着的意义等，他们往往会在这些问题上脱离个人生存的角度，而试图在个人与宏大世界之间建立一种联系。／王　屹

杭春晓／ “70后”，似乎注定了在一种“被规定”和“反规定”的状态中，寻找自己通往世界的路口。这种感觉就像王小波的想象力——绿袖在各个时空中的穿梭。

我们不应该活在一个不真实的描述里，因为那样并不安全。但是，人的内心又总是希望有一种宏大叙事的东西，让我们获得各种情形之所以发生的原因。这是一种很拧巴的状态，却又是“70后”不得不面对的真实际遇。／王　屹

精神建构

杭春晓／ 宏大叙事的东西，背后往往渗透着一种本质主义的“规定”。这种思想，对“70后”的影响也是显而易见的。比如他们一直试图寻找到自己面对世界的通道，这种行为背后，其实还是渗透着强烈的主体意识。

这种主体意识，有时候却是危险的，充满悖论的。 ／王 屹

杭春晓／ 确实。我们用以确认主体性的东西，往往却是他人给我们规定好的。从某种意义上看，一切自认为主体成立的东西，往往都是接受了“非主体”事先通过语言、常识等加以规定好的东西。其中，这种规定，往往还和某种权力塑造有关系。正如我们认为，自己学习雷锋就是好人，但事实上呢，雷锋之所以成为雷锋，是一种权力规定化的结果。

对于这种规定化的东西的怀疑，也是“70后”走向理性的起点。 ／王 屹

杭春晓／ 对。但这里面有种很悖论，但却很真实的东西。一方面，“70后”思维中残余着一些宏大叙事，一些本质主义的东西，并因此时常会带出一些抒情性的、审美主义的东西。但同时，他们却又对这些东西充满了犹疑，对这些东西背后的确定性抱有一种怀疑。这种带有正反两面的思想体验，成为“70后”别具特质的思维方式。

这种东西在精神体验上，呈现为一种质疑性。它往往与坚决的肯定或否定保持着恰当的距离。 ／王 屹

杭春晓／ 这也恰恰正是“70后”与“60后”、“50后”有所不同的地方。他们不像上一代人，有着相对确定的判断立场，或肯定，或否定，甚至是批判，而往往游离在一种中间状态。比如说我们讨论的“70后”艺术家，你仔细体会他们的作品，你就会发现，他们的作品和前面那种非常明显的观点化艺术有所不同。也就是说，你在他们的作品中，很难找到直接而现成的答案。情况往往是，他们更习惯于在视觉显现中表述某种审视的姿态，反思的体验，而非鲜明的立场。

他们的作品中，还非常特出地表现出一种带有不确定感的视觉体验。 ／王 屹

杭春晓／ 是的，无论是画面的形象刻画，还是场景营造，他们的作品往往透出一种或迷失而无所适从的情绪，或带有距离感的审视空间。作为同年人，我非常能够理解这种视觉营造背后的精神空间。

如果对这种精神空间加以界定的话，我想应该是一种质疑主义的理性构建。 ／王 屹

杭春晓／ 这种质疑主义，不是日常经验中的否定性判断，而是悬置了对与错的结果，更加关注结果是如何产生的过程。

其实，这两年流行开来的所谓“忽悠”、“不靠谱”之类的词，背后可能正是这种精神体验。 ／王 屹

杭春晓／ “忽悠”、“不靠谱”，在通俗层面上可以成为一种否定。但我们却能从这些词的背后感受到另外一种东西，因为"忽悠"、"不靠谱"并非要提供另一种结果。从某种角度上，它们也不是一种简单的破坏性否定，而是一种暧昧的否定。虽然，这种暧昧的否定，还不同于我们所说的质疑主义，但或多或少具有一些联系。

“不靠谱”是一个中性词，含义非常丰富。比如说可能一开始是批判对方的不靠谱，是批判权力者说的不靠谱。反过来，你付出努力想要得到的结果，也同样不靠谱，甚至感觉自己也不靠谱。 ／王 屹

杭春晓／ 就这个角度来看，这些词汇的流行，也许正是“70后”生存体验在通俗层面上的一种显现。毕竟，这些词汇流行的背后，正是“70后”正在成为主流年龄段的社会现实。或许，这种流行文化中的某些现象，也正是“70后”倾向于“审视生活”，而非“判断生活”的结果。

审视，是一个过程，而非目标。但今天的社会，却往往喜欢寻找最为简单的操作答案，而非对答案的寻找过程。 ／王 屹

杭春晓／ 而这，或许正是今天重新理解“70后”的价值所在。因为，今天的中国，更需要一种告别“非此即彼”的思维方法。

“非此即彼”的二元对立，往往容易带来简单的对立，并因为对立的情绪找到简单的答案。其实，今天的中国到处充斥着资本，而资本的自我循环力量，往往需要一种权力的构建，无论它是和政治结构联姻，还是和世俗结构联合。而这种权力，往往需要每个人都习惯于简单答案的获取，就像卓别林的电影一样，成为不断转动的社会化机器中的链条，或者说是构件。 ／王 屹

杭春晓／ 这是很可怕的一种现状。缺乏审视过程的答案，往往带来的是一个躁动不安的社会，一个充满乖戾情绪的社会，正如今天网络上流行的谩骂式发泄。无论这种谩骂的立场如何，其实参与谩骂的人，往往在发泄中忽视了一个事实：支撑他们谩骂的信念，可能是没有被他过滤过的，来自于不同结构中的权力意志。

缺乏过滤的观点，并非真正的观点。从这个意义上说，重新讨论“70后”天生的某种质疑主义的精神体验，对于今天的中国，还是有着一种现实价值。或许，今天的中国不再需要王朔的那种“否定”，而是另外一种审视。 /王 屹

杭春晓/ 王朔的“否定”腔，只是曾经具有价值，在今天恰恰是需要警惕的。

对，在那个时代，王朔的“否定”腔，一种出于蔑视姿态的否定，带着一种嘲讽，还是有价值的。因为，那时的环境需要这种东西，来消解某些既定而陈旧了的价值判断。那时，这种反对的姿态，以及这种反对后的带有虚无感的自由，都曾经具有一种改变力。 /王 屹

杭春晓/ 这种改变，在当时具有瓦解某种社会权力结构和控制结构的意义，带有某种思想启蒙的意味。但是今天，它所针对的那种东西早就瓦解掉了，如果还是这种“否定”腔的话，那么可能就真的给这个社会带来痞子味道的动荡。

确实如此。今天我们需要的，不再是对某种“规定”的简单否定，而是对为什么要反对“规定”的思考，对为什么会出现这种“规定”的思考，或者说是这种“规定”何以成为这样的思考。 /王 屹

杭春晓/ 这便是一种理性主义的构建了。但是在中国，这种精神构建是缺乏传统的。无论是中国古代社会，还是近代社会。

中国不像西方，从古希腊的皮浪，到休谟、笛卡尔乃至胡塞尔，有着一条完整的关于怀疑主义，关于质疑精神的思想逻辑。 /王 屹

杭春晓/ 但是中国，要不就是古代的“经典主义”，不容怀疑；要么就是20世纪的“拿来主义”，简单否定后简单肯定。这种土壤中，每一个人都需要被训练为一种既定规范中的人,而非面对“规范”思考的人。

但是,“70后”天然的“不确定”人生，似乎为这种土壤培养了反思者。 /王 屹

杭春晓/ 希望会是这样。我们也能看到一些苗头,正如我们正在讨论的这些艺术家。但是，我们又不得不面对一种现状，“70后”的“不确定”也会在功利主义、物质主义中，成为“油滑主义”的务实性。这不仅是一种可能，还是一种正在发生的状态。

所以，“70后”现在需要的，是对自身特质的自觉。并因为这种自觉，而能成为这个社会中构建理性精神的自觉者。 /王 屹

The Nature of the Indefinite

- How the Seventies Generation Sums up the Experience of Being Alive

A Dialogue between Hang Chunxiao and Wang Yi

Hang Chunxiao / In conceptualizing art of the Seventies generation, popular interpretations fall under the rubrics of "cruel youth" or "cartoon and anime." But in my view, such explications are too simple, or I should say they don't touch the heart of things. The phrase "cruel youth" implies an absurd premise: only people who have been through social upheavals can have an in-depth grasp of society; otherwise one merely enters into fragmentary experiences of their own realm. Maybe artists of the Seventies generation did not live through the kind of intense impacts that their predecessors did, but in their seemingly placid lives they dealt with indefinite circumstances of existence, which gave them chances to take stock of life rationally, and to reflect skeptically on fixed value judgments about life. This is nothing like the narcissism that supposedly comes from suffering a "superficial injury." One could say that the 70s generation, finding itself in an indefinite world, is searching for a path toward a definite vision of the world. Drawing on representative works by different types of 70s generation artists, this exhibition aims to present and explore artistic features that set this group off from previous generations.

Historical Memory

Wang Yi / People of this generation definitely have common ground in terms of what they have lived through. I should say that this is related to overall conditions of an era. For instance, people born in the early 70s, in particular, have memories of major historical events of that decade, and what is more, these memories are unlike those of the previous generation. These were events such as the "Great Leader's" death, the downfall of the "Gang of Four," and the holding of the Third Plenary Session of the Thirteenth People's Congress. Their memories of such events were mediated by symbols, yet they were tied to direct perception. At the outset of the Eighties, as they entered adolescence or youth, reform and opening in our country brought a great mass of fresh cultural forms, along with novel ideas that nobody had time to digest thoroughly. They grew up in a setting where multiple trends were colliding, and survival conditions were such that any given value judgment could prove to be unstable. In the Nineties the tide of economic change had an overwhelming impact. Once again prior memory and experience were flattened and replaced by a new, vulgarized reality. In a sense, with respect to their own lives, there were not many chances to make their own choices; they were washed along as if by a floodtide. There was not much room for initiative; instead, they had to make many adjustments to their own state of being.

Hang Chunxiao / You're right. In our lives we had the right to accept things passively, but not much of a right to make active choices. Yet in the midst of this indefiniteness, we looked for definite ways to cope. Maybe this is what you mean when you talk about making adjustments to one's own state of being.

Wang Yi / There is a paradox here that amidst the indefinite, we are searching for something definite. In my view, this is related to ideas tied to grand narrative that continued to be part of our generation's education. In a certain respect, their earliest intellectual resources were materialist dialectics from Hegel through Marx.

Hang Chunxiao / What is more, this was something that had previously been refashioned by China. It was no longer "original equipment." (Laughter) In fact, during the ensuing years there has been reflection on such things, with attempts to reshape them through other intellectual resources, but this is a long, drawn-out process.

Wang Yi / Without a long process it will be hard to change this. Every entrance examination was accompanied by imposed education of that type, so certain things kept being reinforced. In fact, thinking it over, we can see that the influence of such education is deep-seated.

Hang Chunxiao / Heh-heh. No matter what attempts at restructuring we make, there will be times when such influences pop up. For instance, there is a grand narrative view of history. Now we are attempting to explicate the artistic behavior of the Seventies generation: wouldn't you say that we are falling into just such an intellectual pitfall?

Perhaps. But from another angle, we can still get a feel for things through the particulars of our lives. / Wang Yi

Hang Chunxiao / I am firmly convinced of this point. For instance, as we neared graduation from lower middle school, teachers would encourage us to take the exam for vocational school. Behind such encouragement there were authoritative rulings: that is, after graduating from vocational school there would be a work assignment, which would directly qualify you as a state cadre. You have to realize that in the world view of socialist China, being a state cadre was described as an ideal life. So some classmates accepted this idea. What was the outcome? Looking back on their lives, you'll find that fate played a big joke on them, and behind that joke was a seemingly definite view of survival value. This value collapsed right in front of our eyes, in a directly perceptible way.

Yes, at each crucial point of our growth, people would tell you what you ought to do, and at the time it really seemed that you ought to do it. But before two years had gone by, you would discover the great absurdity of the choice you had made. There is no doubt that such experiences were prevalent in the upbringing of the 70s generation. In our youthful period, after going through several changes like this, a mentality of distrust and doubt would arise in a person's mind, something that was not arrived at by rational reflection. / Wang Yi

Hang Chunxiao / That's for sure. In the coming of age of the Seventies generation, skepticism is an inborn mood.

Take for instance 1976, when Mao Zedong passed away. At that time my family was still being rusticated in a village due to our political background. In my memory, the whole production brigade was one big funeral parlor. Everywhere you looked there were mourning banners bearing the words "Dolefully Grieve for Our Great Leader." Everywhere there were white wreaths and funeral canopies. Dirges were broadcast on loudspeakers in our village, and eulogies were read over and over, recounting Mao Zedong's history. All of us were organized to mourn in unison, and we were in a grief-stricken state. What is more, this state was fully genuine. But in my memory one richly theatrical incident stands out—the production brigade's clerk was so busy writing mourning couplets that when an onlooker came too close to his writing table, the clerk unthinkingly swiped at the man's face with his brush, giving him an opera-style make-up job. Then the two of them looked at each other in frozen disbelief. Right then all the people there burst out laughing, and their grief was instantly replaced by a farcical mood. This left an especially deep impression in my memory, because we had just been in such a state of sorrow, then it turned instantly to farce. / Wang Yi

Hang Chunxiao / Perhaps at the time you could not grasp what that transformation meant, but as you grew up, such an incident would reappear in memory, to be described and understood in a new way.

Such things were common memories. For instance, in the late Seventies and early Eighties I lived in a hutong neighborhood in Beijing. On my way home from netting fish in a canal one day, I found that the alleyways were all deserted. It turned out that Liu Shaoqi's funeral was being shown on television. Actually there were many funerals around that time, and whenever one was held, the streets would be almost deserted. All the people in the courtyard would be clustered around a single television set, watching a funeral. The adults would give commentary for your benefit, talking what a miscarriage of justice had happened, and telling all the things this person had done in his lifetime. / Wang Yi

Hang Chunxiao / There was a feeling of being subverted, a feeling that everything could be turned around and re-explained in a different way.

Yes. Things were all different from what they had been, and everything could be turned end-over-end. What is more, there was a sense of authority in this: whether to negate something or to re-affirm it, both stages were pumped up with authority. As a result of the memories we built up, we gradually adopted the view that it was quite normal for things to be turned this way and that. / Wang Yi

Hang Chunxiao / As a child I lived in a fairly remote mining area, and I have similar memories. For instance, on one hand I would see the slogan "Down with the Traitor Liu Shaoqi" in a certain corner at my school, but on the other hand adults would educate me that Liu Shaoqi was a leader of our Party and our nation—that his good name had been restored. In fact maybe there was no way to understand such a thing, and maybe one did not even thing it mattered. But when you ran into such things constantly while growing up, such memories would become an intellectual resource. They would reappear to influence your judgments. Ultimately you would come to believe that there was hardly anything in this world you could believe in firmly.

Wang Yi / It sounds paradoxical, but it is a fact. For instance, when I learned to sing children's songs in kindergarten, one of the songs went like this: "In ancient times there was a man of the surrender faction; his name was Song Jiang, and he harmed many people. Nowadays there is a man of the imperial faction ..." That song was directed at Zhou Enlai, who was the target of the "Criticize Lin Biao and Confucius" campaign that was then underway. But before long Zhou Enlai passed away, and suddenly Tiananmen Square turned into an ocean of white banners, where people gathered in great numbers to read memorial poems for Zhou Enlai. Soon the Gang of Four fell, and our kindergarten pasted up portraits of the Gang of Four, which children were encouraged to pelt with little bags of sand. The teachers even raised signs and led us marching along the street, shouting the slogan "Down with the Gang of Four." How much of this could a child understand? First we were told one thing, then another. Maybe at the time you just thought it was amusing, but in the process of growing up, this was a key source of doubt that you felt toward anything definitive. The sense of paradox was thrown right in your face.

Experience of Existence

Hang Chunxiao / In 1990 the program Yearning was broadcast, which I believe marked a pivotal point in the lives of the Seventies generation. From that point onward, the influence political topics once had on us began to fade. The overall goal of life soon shifted toward the message in the melody "Peace to All Good People." After that came Deng Xiaoping's "Southern Tour Speech." These things ushered in a change for the Seventies generation, from their youthful, vague idealism of the Eighties to the materialism and pragmatism that came afterwards.

Wang Yi / That shift was not chosen on our own initiative. Rather, it came from forces that emerged as society changed direction, including factors like the groundswell of popular culture.

Hang Chunxiao / Definitely, in our memories of that period, Hong Kong and Taiwan culture was fashionable and on the cutting edge. For example the "Little Tigers" rock band. When they reappeared on stage two years ago for New Years Eve, I wondered why I had been so fond of them in my early years. My liking for them was not just due to youthful enthusiasm: possibly it had to do with our sense of emptiness amidst the overall transformation of society. It seemed that people suddenly had a need for such simple, direct and even superficial things.

Wang Yi / As for popular culture, you have to begin with Teresa Teng. At first we listened to her over short wave broadcasts that were not considered legal. Her music was quite different from the characteristically ethnic or revolutionary music that was available then. It carried a message of individual feelings, not of collectivism.

Hang Chunxiao / Such a message was edifying for anyone who tried to emerge from the constraints of collectivism.

Wang Yi / Back then we may not have been conscious of this in a clear way, but it was a perfect expression of those youthful inner stirrings we felt. It was completely unlike the things that had been instilled into us, which is why it had such special appeal. Later, along with people somewhat older than us, we listened to Cui Jian's "Nothing to My Name." Perhaps we could not understand what lay behind this song as well as they could. But that way of letting your voice pour out freely, giving vent to emotions your yourself did not know the source of—that was a tremendous feeling.

Hang Chunxiao / Even today such a feeling is perhaps an elusive and indefinable mood. Yet it was not completely an individual thing. Somehow it related to a sense of being alive in the society of that era.

Of course. Analyzing that song now, we can say that feeling is a state of spiritual emptiness in a phase of social transformation. People of that period had little, whether we're speaking in terms of employment or stored-up knowledge. Yet it was time to break away from the collectivism they had known, to head toward a phase of independent survival. Thus they felt a confused dread for which they were totally unprepared. Naturally this would give rise to the mood of outcry you hear in "Nothing to My Name." However, for the Seventies generation, this sort of thing may not have seemed so obvious. Yet their youthful phase was surely related in some way to this mood. / Wang Yi

Hang Chunxiao / Unlike the distinct rebelliousness of their predecessors, when it came to the Seventies generation, their rebellion and outcry were mostly elicited by their rapidly changing era, but it was not directed at targets that were all that specific. Thus the Seventies generation began to ponder life amid an outcry that did not have a definite direction.

This is an intriguing kind of outcry. / Wang Yi

Hang Chunxiao / Because the aim of their outcry was not distinct, people of the Seventies generation, once they grew up, became disdainful of results that were specific or clearly defined; instead they preferred to take stock of the process by which results are produced.

There is no way around it. You see, the history we grew up with was filled with results that were constantly being subverted. We could not help adopting a stance of distrusting definite results. / Wang Yi

Hang Chunxiao / This distrust originated in the fact of constant negation.

Back then our parents and teachers all took a negative attitude toward students who flaunted their individuality too early. In shaping us, they tried to inculcate an ideal, collectivized pattern. But for us children the existential reality could not provide that kind of collectivist setting, because everyone was being thrown off their predetermined course by new developments. Our experience of growing up was filled with such paradoxes. I remember that once we heatedly discussed an incident—a university student died while saving a manure-pit worker, but was it a worthy attempt? I remember that we debated this in our political studies class. One side held that the two persons were of equal value, and the opposing side held that their value to society was different. / Wang Yi

Hang Chunxiao / Actually, looking back at such discussions now, I'd have to say that the result is not important. What is important is why we judge things as we do.

That's for sure, but this kind of discussion caused perplexity for our generation—the definite answers we received in our education did not seem to exist in real life. You could say, the maturation of the Seventies generation saw the individual beginning to leave home and try to find spiritual resources in society, but the supposedly definitive spiritual resources of Chinese society just happened to be empty during that period. In that period the whole society, just like the youthful phase of the Seventies generation, was in a phase of "weaning" itself from definitive spiritual resources. / Wang Yi

Hang Chunxiao / Being in this kind of "weaning phase," we sought spiritual help from society, but we seemed powerless to offer anything. As you looked for intellectual resources around you, you would discover that those so-called resources were so indefinite, so vulnerable to upheaval. What you were told a while ago would later be negated. Then you would add your own negation on top of that. You would feel you were being jerked around.

So you would constantly be adjusting your judgments of the world. / Wang Yi

Hang Chunxiao / Many times when I think back, I feel that too many things in my upbringing were off base and indefinite. Often you got used to a certain view of things, but then facts would tell you that your way of understanding things was shaky. For example, I remember in childhood watching films like Tunnel Warfare.[1] I used to feel quite moved that we were surrounded by blessings, while some people in this world still had to live in the midst of "white terror," suffering hellish miseries. But later my life experience convinced me that such thoughts were highly absurd. So naturally one would have to remain wary when faced with all kinds of authoritative didacticism.

It was the same way with imposed collectivism. / Wang Yi

Hang Chunxiao / Yes. During childhood I lived in a mining area: it was a typical industrial settlement in the backward socialist mode. In that mining area we depended on the collective for everything we needed in life. In relation to the collective, we had built up a kind of trust born of dependency. I felt that as long as we were in the collective, we would be secure. But later my father and mother were laid off, one after another. For two or three years they did not even draw wages. Think about it: when you found yourself at loose ends like that, you suddenly find out that the system that had seemed so secure was far from secure. At that time what I read in the media contradicted what I felt in real life. So naturally one would start having doubts about the collective way of doing things. Because of this, I learned to remain wary regarding all authoritative definitions and descriptions.

Experiences of Reading

The sense of distrust that was part our generation's life gave an elusive, unfixed feel to the images of our existence, like those lines from Faust: "Everything before my eyes seems to recede far away; long gone things appear before me one by one." / Wang Yi

Hang Chunxiao / This feeling reminds me of martial arts novels. Back then we could not read such books openly: we always read them on the sly. Actually, looking back, I think adults made too big a deal of it. When children read such things, they merely want to get a taste of fantasy. But back then, in the eyes of parents and teachers, such books were connected with unwholesome social activities, so they were all lumped together and discouraged. It was thought that reading such things was a mark of defiance. But suppression could not control this tendency, and it often led to an opposite result. Suppression enhanced the fascination that those novelistic imaginary worlds held for us.

The reading of the Seventies generation did not seem to have been systematic. It ranged from Zheng Yuanjie's Pipilu to Jin Yong's martial arts books, from the romance novels of Auntie Qiong Yao to the black humor of Wang Shuo, from Gao Jialin[2] to Wang Xiaobo[3], from the Misty Poets of China to Pablo Neruda, from socialism to Sartre: all these things served as reading matter as we dealt with the upheavals around us. What is more, our fragmentary reading of all these things went along with our growth process, as we continually absorbed these things and tried to piece them together. / Wang Yi

Hang Chunxiao / You could also say that there was nothing authoritative in our generation's reading. Especially in their youthful phase, there was rarely anything that could really let them construct a pattern of thinking. Many of my close friends only began to digest their reading, gradually, after their youthful period was passed: only then did they develop their own evaluative stance and attitude. Heh-heh. They are a late-blooming breed, for the most part.

Such late-blooming, omnivorous reading, seen from a certain angle, shows the unstable intellectual core of the whole society's transitional phase. / Wang Yi

Hang Chunxiao / But this kind of rational judgment could not become clear in our early phase of reading. Yet there was always a feeling that something in the text was shaky. For instance when reading Lu Yao's Ordinary World, one could enjoy that somewhat contrived tale of individual struggle, yet one could only half believe what was described in the book. The most obvious example is Tian Xiaoxiao. I felt that she had to die: otherwise the falseness of the father character would have been carried too far. Why do I think this? Because I'll never believe that the Party Chairman of a province would let his daughter have a romance with a worker like Sun Xiaoping. Of course, for people a few years older than myself, such doubts would have been unnecessary.

Yet even as you doubted such things, you could get considerable enjoyment from them. / Wang Yi

Hang Chunxiao / That's right.

In fact, because of their mixed-up reading, members of the Seventies generation could not avoid mixed-up influences from all sides. For instance, even as this generation matures and grows more rational, they cannot help letting contradictory impulses show, such as lyricism or a heroic mentality. Perhaps there is a paradox of individual versus collective which continues to influence the Seventies crowd. / Wang Yi

Hang Chunxiao / This is also expressed as an ambiguous stance with regard to grand narrative. On one hand they try to break away from this mode of thinking, remaining wary of the authoritative mentality behind this mode, but meanwhile they often use this mode in their thinking about issues.

For example, in this dialogue we are trying to formulate a definition of the Seventies generation. Aren't we revealing a tendency toward that same mode of thinking? / Wang Yi

Hang Chunxiao / You have a point: we are liable to veer in that direction. However, we often like to state that the judgments we make are not value judgments, and they are not logical definitions. Rather, they are empirical descriptions. Likewise, we are now trying to engage in description of our life experience, not deliver judgments on it.

It may be so. But the Seventies generation, despite taking such a stance, often goes counter to its original intention. I say this because, in life as we know it, whether consciously or unconsciously, we sense that this pattern of thinking is there. As long as this pattern exists, we keep setting up a construct along the lines it specifies. People of the Seventies generation still hope to use the spiritual resources at their disposal in constructing something that will fit this pattern. Take for instance their ponderings on what it means to be alive—when addressing such issues they often slip away from an individual, existential angle and try to establish a connection between the individual and the macroscopic world. / Wang Yi

Hang Chunxiao / It seems that fate has placed them in a state between acceptance and rejection of imposed "rules," as they search for the crossroads that will connect them to the larger world. This feeling reminds me of what Wang Xiaobo imagines—the character Lüxiu [Greensleeves] shuttling from one temporal realm to another.

We should not live within an inauthentic description, because that would not be safe. However, people harbor some kind of hope for an overall narrative, so they can get a grasp on why situations happen. This is a twisted state of affairs, but it belongs to the circumstances that the Seventies generation has to face. / Wang Yi

Psychic Constructs

Hang Chunxiao / Behind the habit of grand narrative, one often finds that it has been infiltrated by essentialist "rules." The influence of such thinking on the Seventies generation is obvious. For instance, they keep trying to search for an avenue by which they can face the world. But looking behind such behavior, one will find it to have been infiltrated by a strong ideological mentality.

This ideological mentality is at times dangerous, to be sure, and it is filled with paradoxes. / Wang Yi

Hang Chunxiao / Indeed. What we use to confirm our subjectivity is often a rule set by someone else. In a sense, everything that we think was established by subjective consciousness often incorporates, by way of language or common sense, certain rules that were pre-set by something outside of subjectivity. Such rules are often connected to the shaping force of authority. Thus one may be convinced that to act like Lei Feng will make you a good person, but in fact Lei Feng became Lei Feng as a result of rules backed by power.

Skepticism regarding the operation of rules was also the starting point for the Seventies generation to move toward rationality. / Wang Yi

Hang Chunxiao / Right. But there is something quite paradoxical yet also quite genuine in this. On one hand the thinking of our generation has elements of grand narrative in it, certain essentialist traits, from which emerge an aspect of lyricism and aestheticism. But at the same time they are filled with doubt about these things; they are skeptical of the definiteness underlying such things. This experience of thinking both positively and antithetically has become a feature of the Seventies generation's mentality.

As a phase of psychic development, this manifests as a habit of questioning. As a rule, it keeps proper distance both from decisive affirmation and negation. / Wang Yi

Hang Chunxiao / This is precisely where the Seventies generation differs from the Fifties and Sixties generations. We are not like the previous generation, with its relatively definite judgmental stance that negated, affirmed or critiqued. Instead, this generation often slips into an intermediate state. For instance, if you are talking about 70s generation artists, and if you really get a feel for their work, you'll find their works don't show the obvious conceptual thrust of works from preceding generations. That is, in their works you are not likely to find direct, ready-made answers. More often, they are in the habit of representing, by visual means, a posture or stance of evaluation, or a reflective feel, rather than a clear-cut standpoint.

Their works are remarkable for they way they bring out a sense of the indefinite as a visual experience. / Wang Yi

Hang Chunxiao / Yes. Whether in depiction of forms or in establishing a setting, their pictures often reveal a mood of anomie, of not knowing what to do next, or they evoke a sense of distance and space of stock-taking. As one of their contemporaries, I can understand quite well the psychic space behind their visual constructions.

If we want to characterize this kind of psychic space, I would call it a rational construct with a skeptical bent. / Wang Yi

Hang Chunxiao / This skepticism is not the kind of negative judgment we experience in daily life: it is a result of suspending categories of right and wrong, and it is more concerned with the process of how a result arises.

As a matter of fact, this kind of experiential phase may lie behind words like "off base" and "shaky" that have become popular in the past two years. / Wang Yi

Hang Chunxiao / Hang Chunxiao: On a commonplace level, "off base" and "shaky" can have a negative sense, but behind this kind of vocabulary we can get a feel for another meaning because someone who is "off base" or "shakey" is not out to provide yet another fixed result. From a certain angle, this is not simple, destructive negation, but instead is a kind of ambiguous negation. Although such ambiguous negation is not the same as the skepticism we've been talking about, to some degree there is a connection.

"Off base" is a rich world with rich implications. For instance, it may be critical to say someone is off base, as when you might criticize the words of a power holder for being off base. On the other hand, a result you are trying to attain could likewise be off base. You could even feel that you yourself were off base. / Wang Yi

Hang Chunxiao / Seen from that angle, the wide use of such expressions could be a manifestation, on a commonplace level, of what existence is like for the Seventies generation. Behind the popularity of these words is a social reality, namely that the Seventies generation has become the prime age group. Perhaps these popular culture phenomena result from the Seventies generation's tendency to "take stock of life" rather than to pass judgment on life.

Taking stock is a process, not a goal. In today's society, people often like to find the simplest way to manipulate the answer, rather than seeking a process that yields an answer. / Wang Yi

Hang Chunxiao / Herein lies the value, perhaps of coming to a new understanding of the Seventies generation, because in China today we need to bid farewell to the way of thinking that says, "if not this, then that."

The kind of polar opposition that "if not this, then that" can easily lead to simplistic opposition, and oppositional answers often cause one to look for simple answers. Actually, today's China is rife with capital, and the automatic cyclical forces of capital require a construct of power, which may dovetail with the political structure, or it may dovetail with the structures of secular society. This kind of construct needs people to get in the habit of arriving at simple answers, like in the Charlie Chaplin movie, and to become a link or component in the continuously operating social machine. / Wang Yi

Hang Chunxiao / This is a terrible prospect: answers that lack an evaluative process tend to bring about a restless, compulsive society, a society full of perverse emotionalism, as we see on today's Internet, where ranting is a popular habit. Regardless of the stance of such ranting, the people who take part in it are overlooking one thing: the doctrine which supports their invective—which originates in a will to power inherent in a power structure—is not being fed into their reasoning process.

Concepts that do not go through a reasoning process are not concepts. In this sense, there would be real value for present-day China in re-opening the discussion of what the Seventies generation gets at with its innate spirit of questioning. Maybe present-day China does not need the kind of negation the black humorist Wang Shuo was talking about; it needs a different kind of stock-taking. / Wang Yi

Hang Chunxiao / Wang Shuo's negativism had value, but only for a while, and new we need to be wary of it.

You're right. There was a time when Wang Shuo's negativism—that negation born of a disdainful stance—had value due to the message of irony it carried. It had value because the environment then needed something to help dissolve certain fixed, stale judgments. At one time that oppositional stance, and the somewhat vacuous sense of freedom that came afterward, possessed a certain power for change. / Wang Yi

Hang Chunxiao / That kind of change once had an edifying significance in that it shattered certain constructs of social power and control. But now that the things it was aimed at have been shattered, if we continually adopt that tone of negativism, it could bring about a real hooligan-style upheaval.

That is indeed the case. What we need today is no longer simple "negation" of this or that rule. Rather, we need to consider why certain "rules" ought to be opposed; we need to consider why such rules appeared, and why they took the form they did. / Wang Yi

Hang Chunxiao / You are talking about a rationalistic construct, but in China there has not been much of a tradition for psychic constructs of this sort, either in ancient or modern times.

China is not like the West. From Pyrrhon in ancient Greece to Hume and Descartes, right down to Husserl, there has been a complete vein of logical thinking that was concerned with skepticism and raising questions. / Wang Yi

Hang Chunxiao / But in China you have on one hand our ancient "classicism" which brooks no objection, and on the other hand you have our 20th century "gimme-ism." From simple negation we have gone to simple affirmation [of materialism]. In such an environment, every person needs to be trained to fit pre-determined rules, not to face "rules" squarely and ponder them.

But the "indefinite" life-experience of the Seventies generation seems to have provided fertile ground for people who reflect on such things. / Wang Yi

Hang Chunxiao / I hope this is the case. We can see a few budding possibilities, such as the artists we've been discussing. But we have to face the reality that the "indefiniteness" of the Seventies generation, being surrounded by utilitarianism and materialism, will take a pragmatic turn towards "slick-headedness." This is not just a possibility, it is a situation that is now developing.

So what the Seventies generation needs is to realize its own unique characteristics, and thereby become a force for self-awareness which can establish the spirit of rationality in our society. / Wang Yi

---

[1] Didaozhan, a film made in 1965 by PLA Eight One Film Studio, directed by Ren Xudong.

[2] Gao Jialin is the lead character in Lu Yao's 1982 novella Rensheng [Human Life].

[3] Wang Xiaobo (1952-1997) is one of China's most famous post-modern novelists.

王光乐
Wang Guangle

1976年出生于福建松溪，2000年毕业于中央美术学院油画系，是中央美术学院N12艺术团体的创始人之一。2002年开始的“水磨石”和2006年开始的“寿漆”系列作品，将绘画的观念与视觉的呈现，处理为一种冷静的态度，从而在艺术的行为过程中，转化了时间因素，使之成为某种带有参悟色彩的精神体验。这种极具理性色彩的创作方式，向观者提示了一种介于“形式抽象”与“观念表述”之间的精神化审视通道。

Born 1976 in Songxi, Fujian, graduated 2000 from Oil Painting Dept., Central Academy of Fine Arts. Wang was co-founder of N12 Art Group at the Central Academy. In 2002 he began painting his "Terrazo" series, and in 2006 began painting his "Coffin Lacqer" series. He treats the concepts being painted and their visual presentation with a rigorous attitude. Thus in the process of art-as-activity, he converts temporal factors by registering traces that hold colorings of spiritual insight. Such a mode of creation, with its highly rational coloring, opens for the viewer an avenue of reflective awareness between "formal abstraction" and "conceptual representation."

著名电影导演、编剧，1977年生于山西，毕业于北京电影学院摄影系。2006年因导演小成本电影《疯狂的石头》而广受好评，并获多项国内外导演大奖，一时成为炙手可热的“70后”青年新锐导演。2009年作品《疯狂的赛车》以一千万投资成本，取得了过亿的票房成绩，更加奠定了其“新生代鬼才导演”的地位。而今新作《无人区》已拍摄完成，大片《黄金大劫案》也在紧锣密鼓的制作中。

Born 1977 in Shanxi, film director and scriptwriter, graduated from Beijing Film Institute's Cinematography Department. In 2006 he directed the widely acclaimed low-budget film Insane Stones. He is recipient of many directorial awards in China and overseas; he is widely known as a cutting edge director of the Seventies generation. His 2009 film *Crazy Auto Race*, with an investment of ten million, earned a hundred million [RMB] at the box office, securing his position as "wonder boy director" of the new generation. Recently filming has been completed on his new work, *No Man's Land*, and his blockbuster *Gold Heist Caper* is now in production amid great fanfare.

结构承载着观念

王光乐 | 宁 浩

王光乐／ 我小时候感觉到文革的尾巴。在我们那个县城里，文革的标语还有残留。具体的运动虽然过去了，但是文革的意识形态我觉得一直在延续，而且非常强。现在798还会看到文革的标语，今天看起来这些已经变得很有意思。它是文革的形式，但是内容已经被抽取出去了。但我觉得，意识形态只是拐了一个弯，跑到其他地方去了。所谓的文革意识形态，我觉得最直接体现于集体意识，表现在大家的思维方式很单一、趋同，用比较相似的方式去想。我觉得并没有形成个体群：作为一个弱小的声音，独立的声音比较少。然现在比起文革可以发出很多声音了，但是我觉得还是很弱，还是很边缘化。

／宁 浩 对，上世纪70年代人生存记忆中的集体主义，这种东西不仅仅是意识形态上的，而且就是现实生活的单一造成的。70年代，我没什么印象，但80年代是很飞扬的。我出生在工厂，印象中都是比较工业化的一个环境。我应该算是1970年代后期了，完全是红旗下生，蜜罐里长。因为不是出生在文革那个时期，说实话我对此也并不感兴趣，就是大家说起来那些事儿，我也觉得好像跟我没关系，都是过去的事儿了。从我开始记事儿起看到的或比较明显的感受就是变化，从物质上到精神上的几种变化，经历了一个从无到有的过程。你比如说70年代末80年代初的时候，大家都一样，住着分配的那种小房了，都是一种统一的装修制式，审美上面也比较统一，都是绿围墙、水泥地板，都经历了由水泥地板变107，再变地板革、地毯、复合式木地板。

王光乐／ 对，当时全国各地都是那样的地面，满脑子都是绿围墙。小时候睡觉头一转，看到那绿围墙觉得这颜色真土。后来就被淘汰了，城市里又绝迹了。我当时是根据这个记忆一直在画水磨石和绿围墙。你怎么看待创作与生存体验的关联性?

／宁 浩 生活的体验是非常重要的，创作还是要从这种体验出发。它与你个体的结合也是非常重要的，一方面是你看待社会的一种反思，而另一方面也是你看待社会中的自己的反应。你自己该做什么，包括你的责任心，你对社会角色的认识，应该是一个批判者，还是一个建设者等等，必须有一个看待问题的角度。创作者基本上都是从本能出发的比较多，但这个本能是说你在人生或社会的某一个阶段有兴趣，而且有能力去表达的方式。

王光乐／ 我对提纲里提到的“不确定性”挺感兴趣。因为我的命运都是被动的，我没有什么自主选择过，特顺命的。小的时候没有被捆绑，什么都好玩，非常丰富，但是长大了会发现每个人都变得单调了，会被一些意识控制住了。我经常在想，要从这里面跳出来，希望能成为一个比较独立的、能够思考的人，是这么一个状态。

/宁 浩

我觉得“不确定”是所有艺术家的特点，不一定是“70后”的特点。人类的探索精神是一直存在的，这在各行各业的优秀者当中都一样，而且与时代都没关系，它是普遍性的。不确定那是当然了，因为什么东西都是不确定的。以后当然就更不确定了，像“80后”更不确定，他们面临着一个更加严酷的环境，所以，那种不确定性可能要比我们更强吧。谁说自己有特别明确的方向都是扯淡。连朱元璋都说，原本想打家劫舍没成想弄假成真。干那么大的事儿的人都没搞清楚自己的终极目标跟立场，更别说让现在这帮搞艺术的有自己的立场了。

整个从1980年代生活过来，经历了1990年代，再到2000年，这种世界或整个你周围环境的变化与变革是非常剧烈的。因为中国整个是处于一个急速发展和快速变化的过程当中，它所出现的矛盾和生活中所表现出来的戏剧性就是非常充满荒诞色彩的。其实有矛盾吗？就是变化太快了，那在这种情况下它一定会有很多比较有戏剧性或荒诞色彩的事物产生，这个东西是你看得到的，也是我觉得有意思的地方，那就把它拍下来了。

王光乐/

我能体验到你的感受，那种荒诞感在附中的时候就很明显感觉到了。那时候我很喜欢摇滚，一年之后我感觉这样不对，我就在想到底摇滚是什么？我想摇滚精神就是不羁，我只能理解这么多。我会把这种精神放在内心深处，不是很表露出来。当然这还是一种反社会的意味，是蚂蚁可以向大象说不的姿态，现在也一直在作用于我，就是不要变成大象的附庸，做我的小蚂蚁好了。我还是这样一个姿态，只不过我就不会再很朋克的装束而已。你的作品《疯狂的石头》，就表现出很有荒诞的现实感。

/宁 浩

呵呵。我其实在《疯狂的石头》的拍摄阶段是对荒诞主义比较感兴趣，而且在相当长的一个阶段我都对荒诞主义的命题比较有兴趣。你和我好像很不一样，你的画面是比较冷静和细腻的语言。你是中央美院第一工作室的人，为什么没有走向古典油画？

王光乐/

虽然我们接受的是写实性的绘画训练，但老师经常说的是：应该画自己的真情实感。我对这些话就比较敏感。我在画一个人脸的时候，怎么画我都没有感觉。后来我的毕业创作干脆把人都去掉，画了一个黑色的空间，其中有一束光线。因为我觉得自己能力有限，我就收敛起来，用很长时间去画窄窄的一条光，可能会好一点，实际上这就是在画我的真情实感。

/宁 浩

有意思。指导老师同意你的创作么？

王光乐/

我以此为理，跟我们的院长争辩。行不行我觉得无所谓了，我已经找到乐趣了。当时我在画的时候就觉得我找到艺术了，绘画应该是这样。

/宁 浩

我一直以为，艺术实际上对于我或者人类来说，其实和科学是一样的，是一种认知世界的途径。艺术创作本身，实际上也是艺术家自己探索世界和了解宇宙真相的一个过程。在我看来，你画的水磨石就很有超越的意味。

王光乐/

当时画这些水磨石的时候就是想“无我”，忘掉自己。我们每天都会苦恼，这无非就是太在意自己了。我画这些画，其实有种修炼的意味。更多时候我不想有情绪，不想像青春期之前那样心律那么快了，我也不想内心再冲突了，我想把自己放得很淡。当然“无我”并不是没有我了，看怎么去区分。2002年以后，我的画面已经不想有任何叙事了，不想画一个具体对象，因为我发现没有什么事是可以重复说的，就像博尔赫斯所说的，观念和故事等什么都不是，最重要的是“技巧”。他是对小说的一个结构非常感兴趣，结构就要比具体的内容要有普遍性，会恒定，他思考到一个哲学上的问题。我发现我也喜欢恒定的东西，超越时间，终极问题我会感兴趣。

/宁 浩

我的观点很简单，艺术作品的价值就是拿时间来衡量。能够被快速接受的只是一种艺术品，还有一种艺术品是可以历经很多年仍然是非常有价值的。所以也没有什么不对的。至于它能不能够具备穿透性，我深表怀疑。

王光乐/

画面上这种空灵的感觉，实际上还是从阅读中来的，当时读了一些宗教方面的书。我们一直接受唯物论教育，但在我思考问题的时候经常出问题。后来读宗教方面的书，实际上它讲的是唯心，我发现唯心很有意思。当我读到这一类书的时候，就觉得肩上所有物质的东西都可以卸下来，让我很放松。如果物质决定意识形态的话，你会很累，但是意识可以决定物质的时候你发现会特别充实。

/宁 浩

我还是比较看重事情最重要和本质的部分。我不觉得技术是什么最重要的问题，因为这种很多都是表象化的东西。事实就是事实，它摆在那里，你用什么样的信息传递，它还是事实。艺术本质是不变的。现在比较流行“观念绘画”，它所承载的就不是艺术价值了，而是一个情感寄托的价值。它并不是一个能够跨越很长历史阶段的知识。像一些名作，它跨越的历史阶段相对会比较长，流行自然是有它的局限性。在艺术的领域来说，它可能不是个什么特别值钱的玩意儿吧。

Structure Is the Bearer of Concepts

A Dialogue between Wang Guangle and Ning Hao

Wang Guangle / In the county seat back at my home district, there are still remnants of written slogans from the Cultural Revolution. Although the Cultural Revolution as a specific movement has passed, its ideology is continuing, and it is still quite strong. Even now at 798 you can see Cultural Revolution slogans on walls, but the ones we see today have changed in an intriguing way. They have the form of the Cultural Revolution, but their form has been extracted. Yet I feel that the ideology has just rounded a curve and gone to another location. I think the most direct embodiment of Cultural Revolution ideology was a collective mentality, and it was expressed in uniformity, in similar ways of thinking. I feel that a crowd of individuals never managed to form: disadvantaged and independent voices were few in number. Now, as compared to the Cultural Revolution, many voices can be heard, but I feel they are still very weak and marginal.

Ning Hao / That's right. The Seventies generation has memories of collectivism, but it wasn't just an ideology. It was also a matter of uniformity in real life. I do not have any impressions of the Seventies, but in the Eighties everything was in a whirl. I was born in a factory complex, so the impressions I had were of an industrial environment. Actually, I fall into the late-Seventies segment, so "I was born under the red flag and grew up in a honey jar." Because I was not born during the Cultural Revolution, I do not have much interest in that period. When people talk about those events, I feel they are not really connected with me. Those events belong to the past. What I remember earliest—what I first got a distinct sense of—was change, and I'm talking about all kinds of change ranging from material to spiritual. I experienced a process that went from nothing to something. For instance, during the late Seventies and early Eighties, everyone lived in the same kind of small allotment houses, and material goods were fairly scarce. Interiors were done with uniform fittings, and aesthetic design was also fairly uniform. They all had green walls with cement floors. We went through all the stages from cement floors to 107 resin, then to vinyl and rugs and composite wood flooring.

Wang Guangle / Right. Those floor coverings were used nationwide. With our eyes closed we still saw those green walls. When I was lying in bed as a child I would turn my head and see a green wall, and I would think what a drab, countrified look it had. Later green walls were phased out, and you never saw them in the city. I kept painting terrazzo and green walls according to my early memories. What about you? How do you view the connection between life experience and creative work?

Ning Hao / Life experience is very important. What you live through is the point of departure for your creative work. It is important to integrate it into your individuality. On one hand this is a reflection of how you deal with society; on the other hand it is your response to how you deal with your society. What you ought to do, including your sense of responsibility, your grasp of your role in society, whether you practice critique or constructive action—in all these respects you need your own perspective on the issues. Most creative people basically start with their own instincts, but even instincts presuppose that you are fascinated by a certain phase of human life or society, and that you are able to come up with an expressive means.

Wang Guangle / I'm pretty interested in the idea of "indefiniteness" that was mentioned in the outline. Because I have been fairly passive with respect to fate, I have not usually made choices on my own; I have been fairly submissive. When little, I never had my arms and legs tied. Everything was amusing and full of richness. But in adulthood one discovers that people change and act in humdrum ways; they all become controlled by this or that mentality. I wish I could extricate myself from this; I hope to become an independent person and think for myself. That is the state I am in.

/ Ning Hao

I think that being "indefinite" is a characteristic of all artists, not necessarily of Seventies generation artists. The human spirit of exploration has always existed, and this is true of gifted people in all fields. What is more, it is not related to the era, it is universal. Indefiniteness is a matter of course, because things are going to turn out in indefinite ways. In the future they'll be even more indefinite. They will be more indefinite for the Eighties generation, because that generation faces an even tougher environment, so the indefiniteness is perhaps more formidable that what we're dealing with. Anyone who says he has a really distinct direction is full of bullshit. Even Zhu Yuanzhang said that he didn't set out to found the Ming dynasty: he just thought he would do some raiding and pillaging, but later the illusion turned into a reality. Even the doer of such great deeds hadn't figured out what his ultimate aim or standpoint was. So how can you expect this bunch of artistes to have their own standpoint?

I lived through the whole decade of the Eighties, and I went through the Nineties. When it got to 2000, the changes in the world, in your surroundings, became quite drastic. China as a whole was suddenly going through rapid developments, changing with great velocity. The contradictions that emerged, the dramas that were enacted in our lives, had a tremendous coloring of absurdity. Can one really say they were contradictions? I'll just say that the changes came too fast, and they created conditions in which many absurd, dramatic things had to happen. You see all these things in front of you, and they strike you as interesting, so they are worth catching on film.

Wang Guangle /

I can get a sense of what you're talking about. Such absurdity was an obvious feeling for me when I was at the Affiliated Middle School. At the time I was fond of rock music, but after a year of that, I felt it was not right for me. I asked myself what rock music was all about. I felt that its spirit was to be unrestrained—that was as far as I understood it. What I wanted was to incorporate that spirit into my inner life, not display it on the surface. Of course there was an intention to oppose society, the stance of an ant that says no to an elephant, and even now that has an effect on me. That is, I don't want to become a subaltern of the elephant: I can do fine going about my life as an ant. This is my stance, but I don't dress up like a punk any more.

Your piece "Crazy Stones" also expresses the feeling of an absurd reality.

/ Ning Hao

Heh-heh. As a matter of fact during the shooting of "Crazy Stones" I was pretty interested in absurdism. What is more, I've been interested in the premise of absurdism over a fairly long period. You and I are seemingly quite different: your pictures are dispassionate and done in painstaking language. You studied in Studio #1 in Central Fine Arts Institute. Why didn't you develop toward classical painting?

Wang Guangle /

Although we received training in realist painting, our teachers often said to us: you should paint your own genuine feelings. I was fairly sensitive to what they said. When I painted human faces I felt nothing, no matter how I tried to paint them. Later in my creative work I got rid of human subjects and simply painted dark space with a ray of light going through it. I felt my ability was limited, so I retrenched and spent a long time painting just that narrow beam of light, thinking that I could get it right. In fact I was painting what I really felt.

/ Ning Hao

That's interesting. Did your faculty advisor agree to your way of working?

Wang Guangle /

I stood up for myself in a discussion with the Institute's Director. Whether it worked out or not didn't matter: I had found pleasure in it. Back then while painting I felt that I had found art, that this was how I should paint.

I've always felt that art in relation to me, or to human beings, is much like science. It is an avenue for understanding the world. Artistic creation is actually a process of exploring the world, of trying to grasp the true form of the cosmos. In my view, the terrazzo you painted had a transcendent message. / Ning Hao

Wang Guangle / Back then when I painted terrazzo, I wanted to be "egoless," to forget myself. Every day we taste misery, and a big part of it is caring too much about ourselves. In painting those pieces, the intent was to cultivate myself. More often, I just wanted to be done with emotionalism; I didn't want to live with the rapid heart rate I had during my youth. I didn't want to have conflicts deep in my mind; I wanted to be more detached. Of course being egoless does not mean that the "I" does not exist any more. It depends on how you draw distinctions. After 2002 I did not want to have any more narrative in my paintings. I did not want to paint concrete subject matter, because I discovered that nothing can be uttered over again. It is like what Borges said: concepts and story lines don't matter; the important thing is "technique." He was interested in the structure of a piece of fiction, and he considered that to be more universal, more enduring than specific content. His thinking touched upon a philosophical issue. I discovered that I also liked enduring things that go beyond time. I have an interest in ultimate questions.

My viewpoint is very simple. The value of an artwork is measured by time. What can be quickly accepted is just one kind of artwork, but there is another kind that holds a great deal of value even after many years. There's no right or wrong in things people try, but I am skeptical as to whether artworks can show a force that penetrates through time. / Ning Hao

Wang Guangle / The negatively capable space in my pictures actually comes from my reading. Back then I was reading religious books. We received a materialist education, but in thinking over issues I found that this often led to problems. Later I read religious books that espouse idealist thought. I discovered that idealism is quite interesting. While reading books like that, I could unburden myself of all the materialist weight that was on my shoulders. It helped me feel at ease. If material things determine ideology, this can become tiring, but when consciousness determines material things, you feel an inward sufficiency.

All in all I tend to emphasize the important, essential part of things. I do not think that technique is the most important thing at all, because technique is often a matter of representation. Facts are facts: you cannot get around them, and regardless of what information is used to convey them, they are still facts. The essence of art is unchanging. The "conceptual art" that is popular now is not a vehicle of artistic value; rather, its value lies in the release of emotional energy. It is not a form of knowledge that can span a long historical period. Popularity naturally has its own limitation. In the domain of art, flashy novelty in the end may not really count for much. / Ning Hao

寿漆090526　2009年　布上丙烯　116cm × 114cm

Coffin Paint 090526　2009　acrylic on canvas　116cm×114cm

寿漆110706　2011年　布上丙烯　146cm × 146cm

Coffin Paint 110706　2011　acrylic on canvas　146cm×146cm

无题070812　2007年　布上丙烯　180cm × 140cm

Untitled 070812　2007　acrylic on canvas　180cm×140cm

无题100910　2010年　布上丙烯　280cm × 180cm

Untiled100910　2010　acrylic on canvas　280cm×180cm

王 颉
Wang Jie

1978年出生于天津。2008年毕业于中央美术学院油画系，获硕士学位，是中央美术学院N12艺术团体的创始人之一。王颉的画面，多笼罩着某种阴沉而不确定的背景，加之没有人物的衣物，共同构建出一种非时间意义上的场景。而于此种场景之中，主体被虚拟为空洞的图像寓意，显现了艺术家对于生存际遇的自我审视姿态。

Born 1978 in Tianjin, graduated 2008 from Oil Painting Dept., Central Academy of Fine Arts, was co-founder of the N12 Art Group at Central Academy . Wang Jie's canvases, portraying clothes sans wearers enveloped by a gloomy indefinite backdrop, evoke settings that carry an a-temporal message. In such settings, subjectivity is virtualized as hollow visual suggestions, revealing the artist's stance of self-examination amid the circumstances of life.

王 颉
Wang Jie

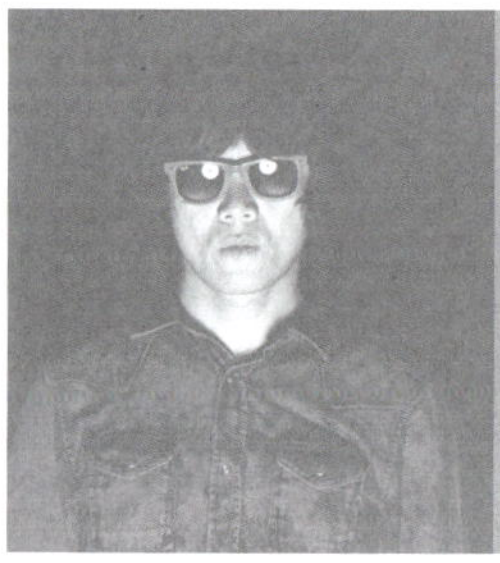

沈黎晖
Shen Lihui

清醒乐队主唱，1997年12月创办摩登天空（Modern Sky），并出版清醒乐队首张专辑《好极了！？》。先后创办Badhead、M2、Guava、LUDI、无花果、过载等唱片厂牌，目前已出版唱片150余张。先后创办《摩登天空》和《听》有声音乐杂志。2007年创办“摩登天空音乐节”，并在美国纽约成立全资子公司——摩登天空美国公司(Modern Sky USA)。2009年创办“草莓音乐节”、“ZOO电子音乐节”、“Fat Art艺术展”。2010年举办“草莓”、“草莓西安”、“长城探戈坞森林”、“摩登天空”等音乐节，摩登天空已成为目前中国最大音乐节运营机构。

Lead singer of "Qingxing Band," founded Modern Sky Productions to publish his band's first album *Haojile*; later went on to publish over 150 albums under the labels Badhead, Guava, Ludi, Passion Fruit, and Overload. In 2007 founded *Modern Sky* and *Listen* magazines. In 2009 produced "Strawberry Music Festival," "Zoo Art Festival," and "Fat Art Expo." In 2010 produced music festival such as "Strawberry," "Strawberry Xi'an," and "Great Wall Tanglewood." His Modern Sky has become the largest producer of music festivals in China.

历史和时间只不过是假设

王 颉 | 沈黎晖

沈黎晖／ 你会不会觉得画画不过瘾？就是说在这么一个被限制的空间里做东西。

／王 颉 我通常需要先确立一个概念或课题，在不同的阶段试验新的语言变化。先把概念里面的事做到位了，再把这个框打开，进入下一个空间。绘画有时像是在面壁，面对一个空空的平面，把它变成一个世界，有一种从无到有的创造乐趣。

沈黎晖／ 我觉得这种创作肯定是理性的。

／王 颉 或许是相对的、局部的理性吧。从创作方法上看是的，先形成一个概念，形式语言和技术手段围绕观念展开，作品局部是逻辑的、严密的。但从作品整体上看我建构的又是非逻辑的、不真实的、荒诞的。我的思考也是非系统化的、不确定的，不相信任何意义的本源及其真实性，似乎又是非理性的。

其实理性主义是当代艺术的特殊话题。启蒙时代理性曾帮助人们脱离愚昧荒蛮，了解自然，但在工业革命浪潮中，科技理性推动的标准化、统一化成为社会主导，人文理性在人们对科技进步的片面追求中日趋边缘化，人权、自由、平等都成了空谈。人的生活几乎完全被自己创造出来的科学和机器控制，人的异化问题产生了。60年代席卷世界的“左翼革命浪潮”和70年代以福柯为代表的后结构主义，都是对之前问题的不同回应。揭示异化、反对异化也成为艺术的重要研究课题，这其中包含了很多对理性主义的反思和批判。

但中国有更特殊的情况。如果说文革是整个社会非理性的顶峰的话，那么在接下来的80年代，虽然社会秩序得到调整，但左翼革命式的激情状态在文化艺术方面却表现出很强的惯性。在交替上演的艺术运动中，人们用一种东西打倒另一种东西，喊口号争话语权的表演随处可见。直到近些年这种惯性才被渐渐削弱——很少时代性的艺术运动，似乎是一盘散沙，少了些浮躁和喧嚣，艺术更趋向于个人语言的体系建构，似乎从对立、对抗走向更多元化的局面。与之前相比这个时代的艺术具有更多的理性特征。

沈黎晖／ 现在表达的渠道变多了，反而让大家有了更多发生的可能。没有以前的完全对立，这跟音乐很像。美术和音乐，仍然是一代人的记忆。每个时代就要有对应的美术和音乐。美术是有激情的，它也必须有激情。可是音乐必须经过严密的排练和配合，它是特别理性的，而在台上呈现时需要特别激情，是在有限制的规则下做现场的提升。与你的创作的过程可能是差不多的。

／王 颉 是的，视觉艺术恰恰也需要通过严密的技术控制、整合表达复杂变幻的感觉世界，是理性和感性反复打造的过程。

沈黎晖／ 美术还是更偏个体的，而音乐则需要太多人的配合。

/王 颉

艺术家个人可以对绘画有绝对的控制力。但对于摇滚乐来说，资金、团队和技术设备都直接影响作品。“星星美展”当年没场地，作品也可以挂公园里展。但音乐最少要有设备和场地，它所要考虑的东西和绘画还是有很大的差别。

沈黎晖/

我以前在美校受到的教育都是很传统的，最多讲到印象派。但当时有个老师给我们看埃舍尔的作品，就把我们的想法都颠覆了：原来还可以这么想。我当时特别感谢这样的老师，把我们班最传统的学生都激发出来，让他们重新颠覆一个东西，去重新看待一个事物。后来我就非常喜欢超现实的风格，像马格利特、契里科、达利等。我觉得我内心还是挺阴暗的，所以我会去喜欢这些东西。可是我觉得生活的这个时代就是一个阴暗的时代，充满污染的时代，后来我们写了很多相关的作品。

我觉得我们这个时代就是受到污染的时代，做美术、做音乐最早接受到的这个世界给予的讯息就是这样。我们每个人就是一个介质，接收着环境中负面的东西。因为敏感，所以比别人吸收得更快，如果传达出来的是有感而发的真实的话，自然也就传达出来这样的情绪。像我们现在为什么没有去画那特别古典的东西，因为我们现在没有这些东西，没有让你真正放松的环境。

我之所以对神秘主义感兴趣，就是因为小时候生活在一个特别超现实的环境。当时我们的小学在一个悬崖上，底下是一条臭水沟，因为上游是东方红炼油厂。学校的另一边全是草地和树林，特别自然的环境。我们都在草地里跑，看到各种各样的野草。我就记得看见一个小水塘，里面全是虾和鱼，特别安静，突然感觉像发现了一个秘密世界的入口一样，可是后来我再去的时候就找不到那个水塘了。我觉得我就是在寻找记忆中的那个东西。那个时候你就会感觉那边是工业，而这边才是我们应该过的生活。也就是为什么现在绘画或艺术变成了这样，如果你是发自内心的，那就一定是准确的，就像一个时代的镜子。音乐就是一个镜子，不加修饰，真正好的作品你看起来是主观的、是无意识的，却是最真实的。70年代我觉得就是污染的、工业时代的记忆。这是一种潜藏的记忆。你的作品也包含着一种历史的意识。

/王 颉

在作品里我会借助某些历史意象表现时间和生命，但我一直认为艺术本质上是关于时间的，每个时代的艺术都用不同的方式回应关于时间的命题。而我需要一种特殊的形式表现时间里“人的存在”，并且是艺术史之前没有的方式。我选择了去除人的可视肉体只保留衣装的观念语言。面对时间的无限，肉体的常规形式在画面中可以被超越，“空”与“无”能够最大限度、最本质地表现“有”。在中国哲学里 “有”与“无”是可以相互转换，生命既是有形的也是无形的。

其实在画面上隐去肉体的想法在美院时就开始了。因为从附中到美院的学习基本上是头像、半身像、人体写生课程的重复，乏味的学院教育体现的是西方传统美术史的趣味，而西方美术史也是一部人体肖像的视觉史。受这种教育影响的当代艺术也自然会是脸的艺术、肉体的艺术的泛滥。我想要对学院教育和艺术史做一些离经叛道的事，这个观念或许满足了我当时的某种“叛逆心理”。另一方面，在这样一个网络信息时代，我感到人与人之间的主体差异越来越小，人们更关注可以标志和辨认的外在空壳。在奇丽光鲜的个性化服饰下，身体和灵魂也许是空洞和苍白的。因此我把没有人的衣装作为对这个时代的隐喻，一切外在的繁华喧嚣都要留给时间的凝固。

沈黎晖／ 谈到时间，我觉得时间就是用来耽误的，我们现在做的所有事情都是在消磨时间而已。自己找到一个有乐趣的消耗时间的方式就行了。人很短暂，肉体会消失，实际上这衣服很快也会消失，只不过是时间长短的问题。我的世界观认为这个世界本身就是一个游戏，所有的东西都会消失。我们现在生活就是一个虚拟的数字世界。通过科技的积累，我们局部破解了我们的世界的秘密。悲哀的是，没有人能逃脱，与编程员（造物主）抗衡。我们的智慧是无法得到这个真理的全部的，我们只能得到一个片段而已。当然我们还得乐观，好处就在于你不会骄傲。因为你不过是游戏里的一个角色。同时也不会太悲观，因为你能把我怎么样呢，反正我也就是一游戏里的角色。古人没那么多杂念，最接近这个游戏的规则。当我们静静地躺在地上，呼吸真正好的空气，望着星空，跟大地和整个游戏融为一体的时候，那个时候给你的信息反而是最接近真理的信息。而这个东西我们现在越来越少了，尤其是生活在城市里面。我觉得这个世界看起来是那么的不确定，但是其实所有东西都是确定的，因为在这个游戏里所有的程序都是编辑好了的。我倒觉得这个世界看起来很混沌，确实游戏也有无限可能的结局，但它就是一个游戏啊。从这个角度讲，我觉得又没有什么是不确定的，所有事情都是确定的，看起来混沌而已。

／王　頔

从大的方面讲，我确实看不到什么意义，一个人做的只是在做一个局部或碎片的东西。我唯一能确定的是我对很多既定说法的怀疑。我的作品中如果涉及历史图像和社会符号，这些仅仅是提供的一些视觉片段和思维材料。历史有真实性，但我们所能触及的历史都只是一种假设，是经过加工的、被误读的“伪史”，得不到真相。因此通过对历史符号的借用，能够产生更精彩的想象空间对于我更重要。不是怀疑道德，而是怀疑既定的、统一的道德；也不是不要真理，而是会假设有不同真理的可能性。这是我比较赞同的。我有些作品会构建历史的语境，紧张、暴烈，但在最冲突的时刻化为一种孤寂，灰飞烟灭，人的肉体都不见了，只有追逐的衣装，在时间面前，历史和人生显得格外荒凉和好笑。

很多人会觉得“70后”生活在一个很安全的年代，但对于我来说并不存在所谓的安全感。很多社会大动荡距离我们太近，我把这些动荡比喻成是一次次核爆炸，它的辐射是向外弥漫的，我出生的年代即使是身体上没有受到直接伤害，但我们这一代仍会被“辐射”到。记得有一个画面，小学时边看着电视里的《变形金刚》边做作业，作业大多是为套话连篇的作文找中心思想或是不切实际的应用题，窗外传来的是80年代中国处处兴建项目的工地轰鸣，偶尔会听到父母提到一些事情，说到某某同事在文革的经历，有些又欲言又止。这些记忆混杂在一起既真实又虚幻。我觉得60、70、80年代有很多问题是相似的。

沈黎晖／ 对，我真没觉得那么强的差别。我们拿十年作为时间点来谈，相对于历史可能就是一秒钟而已。不可能有那么大的差异，我觉得现在的很多东西都是一直存在的。

很多本质的东西没有改变，也没有度过，一个大的时代跳过去了吗？ ／王 颉

沈黎晖／ 所以最安全的就是知道自己是一个游戏里的角色，其他什么都不重要。那么多主义、知识，没用的，所有的知识都是片面的，就是盲人摸象，宗教都是这样。我们就可以自由自在一点，自然地去接受一些知识。我们所做的就是创造一些所谓的事情，似乎是一种牢不可破的信誉，但是所有的一切都非常脆弱。在这样一个短暂的游戏时间里，就不要给自己设定太多的障碍，每一本书里的知识可能都会变成发现真理的障碍。我们要回到原点，就是游戏里的一个角色。其实就是用你自己认为正确的方式去浪费掉游戏的时间。人生就是这么一点事。

先秦时期的思想家感觉更容易接近真理，也就是中国哲学的"道"。我们现在耗费太多精力是在解决我们自己制造的衍生的问题。似乎科学在进步，但这些问题并不是最根本的。 ／王 颉

沈黎晖／ 实际上以前已经把这个题解了，现在是人类给自己设定了新的方式，新的问题随之而来。人很大部分是在处理新来的问题，反而是把人与这个游戏的最根本关系忽略了。相比古代可能没有任何的进步，只是不断地发现和印证。这个世界不是我们自己创造出来的，可能越到后来越觉得这个世界就是一个游戏。

History and Time Are Only Hypothetical

A Dialogue between Wang Jie and Shen Lihui

Shen Lihui / Do you sometimes feel that painting is not enjoyable enough? I mean you are creating something in a limited space.

/ Wang Jie

Wang Jie: Usually I need to establish a concept or theme so I can try new language changes at different stages. I need to finish what dictated by the concept before I can open this frame and enter into another space. Sometimes painting is like facing the wall in meditation. You look at a blank planar surface and try to make a world out of it. There is the fun of creating something out of nothing.

Shen Lihui / I believe that such art production is a rational process.

/ Wang Jie

Maybe it is relative, partial rationality. It is rational in terms of the method used: a concept is established and then forms unfold and techniques are used around this concept. Details of a piece of work are logical and carefully produced. Yet taken as a whole, the construction of my paintings is illogical, unreal, and absurd. My thinking is unsystematic and unfixed and tends to be irrational because I do not believe in the source or truthfulness of meanings.

In fact, rationality is a special topic of contemporary art. In the age of the Enlightenment, rationality helped man to stay away from ignorance and savageness and to understand nature. During the industrial revolution, however, standardization and uniformity as promoted by technological rationality played leading roles in society, and humanistic rationality was gradually marginalized as a result of man's pursuit after technological progress. The ambition to achieve human rights, freedom, and equality became sheer empty talk. Man's life was almost completely controlled by technologies and machines he created. Thus the issue of human alienation arose. The leftist movements that rocked the world in the 1960s and the post-structuralism represented by Foucault in the 1970s responded to the issues of an earlier period. To disclose and resist alienation became an important task of art, and that included a great deal of reflection and critique on rationalism.

The situation in China was quite unique. The Cultural Revolution marked the peak of irrationality in society. In the 1980s, leftist passion exhibited its strong momentum in culture and art, although social order had been partly restored. In successive art campaigns, people used one thing to overthrow another, and there were fights everywhere for the right of discourse. The momentum of these has ebbed in recent years. Epoch-making art movements are rarely seen now, and the art community seems to have fallen apart. There is less sound and fury, and art development tends to be more focused on the structuring of personal languages. Oppositions tend to be replaced by pluralism. Compared to the previous period, art of today has assumed more rational attributes.

Shen Lihui / With increased channels for expression, everyone has more possibilities for creativity. As is the case in music, there are no longer the outright oppositions in fine arts that there used to be. Fine arts and music continue to hold the memories of each generation, and each generation has its favorite art and music. Fine arts are passionate and they need passion. Music is highly rational because it involves close cooperation and strict rehearsing. Yet it must be passionate on the stage: this is a live enactment of sublimation within the framework of given rules. This may be similar to the process of your creative work.

/ Wang Jie

Yes, that's true. Visual arts also need strict technical control to represent the complicated and ever-changing sensuous world. This is a process where both rationality and sensibility are at work.

Shen Lihui / Fine arts are mostly personal while music often involves the cooperation among a number of individuals.

/ Wang Jie

An artist can have absolute control over his painting. A rock 'n' roll music piece, however, is directly influenced by funding, the band, equipment, and technology. The Star Group Show was set up in a park because an indoor venue had not been secured. A concert cannot be held without equipment and a concert hall. The factors involved in music are quite different from those in painting.

Shen Lihui /

The education I received at the art school was quite traditional and the course content never went beyond impressionism. Yet our understanding of art was drastically changed when a professor showed us Escher's drawings: the world could be viewed in a quite different way! I was particularly grateful to that professor for enabled even the most devout followers of traditional painting question what they believed and look at things from a new perspective. Later I came to love surrealistic paintings, such as those by Magritte, Chirico, and Dali. I thought there was a gloomy side in my heart and that was why I liked those paintings. Yet I also believed that ours was a gloomy time, a time of pollution. Later we produced many similar works.

I think this is a time of pollution. This is the first message the artists and musicians received from the world. Each of us is a conductor that receives negative things from its environment. We are more absorbent than others because we are more sensitive. If what we express comes from our hearts, it is also mixed with such negative emotions. Now we do not paint classical paintings because we do not see those images in our daily life and we do not have a relaxing environment.

I am interested in mysticism because I lived in a "surrealistic" environment when I was a child. The primary school I attended was located on a cliff with a foul-smelling river beneath it, because the Dongfang Refinery was located on the upper reach of the river. On the other side of the school were meadows and forests that formed a natural environment. We ran on the meadows and saw trees and grasses of various kinds. I remember there was a pond teeming with small fish and shrimps. The pond was very quiet and I suddenly felt as if I had discovered the secret entrance of a world. Yet the pond was no longer there when I went back again later. I think I have been looking for what is buried deep in my memory. I felt that on one side of the cliff was industry and on the other was the life we wanted to live. That explains why my paintings look as they do. What comes from your heart is precise; it is like a mirror for the times. Music is a mirror, with no decorations added. Good works appear to be subjective and unwitting, but they are real and true. I think that memories of the 1970s are filled with pollution and industry. Such are latent memories. Your works also contain a sense of history.

/ Wang Jie

I use some historical images to represent time and life in my paintings, but I always believe that art itself is about time. Art of different times responds to propositions about time in different ways. I want to represent "man's being" in time in a unique way, an approach that has never been used in art history. I have chosen the conceptual language in which visible human bodies are gone with only their clothing left behind. In the face of infinite time, the usual state of man's body can be transcended in painting. "Being" can be best represented by "emptiness" and "nothingness" in a most fundamental way. In Chinese traditional philosophy, "being" and "nothingness" are interchangeable, and life is both physical form and formlessness.In fact, I began to consider taking the human body away from my paintings since my college years. I studied head portraits, busts, and human figure sketching in the Institute and its affiliated middle school. Western art history is a visual history of the human body. Traditional Western art comprised the major part of the boring training I received at the academy. It is natural that, under the influence of such training, contemporary art is all about human faces and bodies. I want to do something that runs counter to academic education and art history. Taking the human body away from my paintings fits in with my "rebellious mentality." On the other hand, the difference between individuals is diminishing in the information age. People care more about identifiable and distinguishable appearances while the body and soul beneath their flashy, individualized clothing may be insubstantial and empty. That's why I use dancing clothes as a metaphor for our time: all flamboyancy and commotion will be solidified over time.

Shen Lihui /

Talking about time, I think it is meant to be killed. All that I have been doing is nothing more than killing time. It's fine as long as you can find an interesting way to kill time. Life is transient and our flesh will disappear. So will our clothes. It is just a matter of time. I think the world itself is just a game, and everything will disappear in the end. Now we are living in a virtual, digital world. We have partly solved the mysteries of the world thanks to technological advances, but it is a woeful fact that no on can escape from or fight against the programmer (the Creator.) Our human wisdom can never enable us to understand the truth in its entirety; we can only get glimpses of it. Of course we should also look at the bright side of it: we don't feel arrogant because we are just common players in the game. We won't be pessimistic either, because things cannot be any worse for us minor game players. People in ancient times were free from the many distracting thoughts and they followed the game rules to the letter. We are closest to truth when we lie on the ground quietly to breath fresh air, look at the starry sky, and become one with the earth and the game. But we are spun farther and farther away from that, especially when we live in the city. This world seems to be so uncertain, but in fact all things are certain and fixed, because all programs in this game have been written. This world looks chaotic because the possibilities of how it will end are infinite; it is just a game. So I don't see anything that is uncertain. All things are fixed; they just appear to be chaotic.

Generally speaking, I don't see any meaning. One is just working on a detail or fragment of something larger. What I feel sure of is that I have doubts about many propositions. My paintings include many historical icons and social symbols, but these are nothing more than visual fragments and materials for thinking. History is true, but the historical truths I can access are only postulates or processed and misinterpreted pseudo-history. I cannot arrive at true history. For me, it is more important that I can create more fantastic imaginative spaces by using historical symbols. It's not that I have doubts on morality but that I do not subscribe to formulated moral codes. It's not that I turn my back on truth but I believe in the possibility of different truths. Some of my paintings provide historical contexts which are tense and violent. Yet they change into solitude or disappear at the climax of conflicts. The human bodies are gone and the clothes that are left behind are chasing one another. In the face of time, history and life appear to be particularly desolate and absurd. / Wang Jie

Many people tend to believe that those born in the 1970s lived in a safe time, but I don't feel any sense of security. We have been so close to so many social upheavals. I think of these as radioactive atomic explosions: we were not directly injured, but we are still within their radiation range. When I was a kid, I used to watch Transformers while doing my homework, which was mostly about summarizing the themes of given texts and meaningless mathematic calculations which were designed as exercises to handle practical issues. Machines of a construction site roared outside the window, and sometimes I overheard the conversation between my parents. They would start talking about what happened to one of their colleagues during the Cultural Revolution, but stop the conversation before they barely started. These are mixed in my memory; they seem to be both real and illusory. I think that people in the 1960s, 1970s, and 1980s shared many similar problems.

Shen Lihui / That's right. I didn't see any big difference either. We use the decade as a basic unit of time, but it may be just a second in history. There cannot be substantial difference: many problems have continued to exist.

Many fundamental things have not changed or passed. Has a great era just skipped on past? / Wang Jie

Shen Lihui / So the safest thing is to know that one is playing a role in the game. Nothing is important except that. The many philosophies as well as the bulk of knowledge we have are useless. The knowledge we have is partial. We are just like the blind men feeling the elephant. This is the same case with religions. We should act more freely and get knowledge in a natural way. What we have been doing is to create something that seems to be credible without doubt. In fact, everything is so fragile. In such a short game time, one should not create too many obstacles for himself. The knowledge contained in each book may become obstacles to truth. We need to get back to the starting point for our players' roles. Life is about how to use up game time in what you believe to be the right way.

Thinkers before the Qin Dynasty were closer to the truth or Dao of ancient Chinese philosophy. Now we spend too much time trying to solve the problems we created for ourselves. We seem to be making scientific progress, but these are not the fundamental questions. / Wang Jie

Shen Lihui / In fact, this problem was solved in the past. We are facing new problems because we have created new approaches for ourselves. We are dealing with new problems most of the time to the extent that we have neglected the basic relations between us and the game. Compared with our ancestors, we have not made any progress. We are constantly discovering and conforming to what has been discovered and confirmed. We did not create this world, and we may be more inclined to look at it as a game as time goes by.

奔跑的身体 No.1　2009年　布面油彩丙烯　220cm × 200cm

Running Body No.1　2009　oil & acrylic on canvas　220cm×200cm

奔跑的身体 No.2　2009–2011年　布面油彩丙烯　220cm × 450cm

Galloped Body No.2　2009-2011　oil & acrylic on canvas　220cm×450cm

浮生 No.2　2010年　布面油彩丙烯　220cm × 355cm

Floating Lives No.2　2010　oil & acrylic on canvas　220cm×355cm

被唤醒的聚会　2011年　布面油彩丙烯　200cm × 450cm

Party was Awaked　2011　oil & acrylic on canvas　200cm×450cm

尹朝阳
Yin Chaoyang

1970年出生于河南南阳，1996年毕业于中央美术学院版画系。尹朝阳对油画语言的体验，无疑充满了个体化的激情。他早期带有英雄欲望的梦幻现实主义结构，与这种语言张力统一，成为别具感官冲击力的图像谱系，将70年代生人所具备的迷茫、执著及其内心的不安、躁动，表达为一种充满力量的破坏与探寻未知的精神语境，是中国剧烈变革期成长起来的一代青年的特殊化形象呈现。尹朝阳十多年来不断变化的创作，从某种角度上看，正代表了通过教育获得理想主义的“70后”，在成长中被现实抽离理想内核后的自我寻找与自我塑造。

Born 1970 in Nanyang, Henan, graduated 1996 from Printmaking Dept., Central Academy of Fine Arts. His sense of oil painting language is filled with unmistakable personal passion. At first his work was informed by a magical realist structure of heroic desire, integrating the tensions of such language into a sensorily shocking typology of image-forms. Drawing on the anomie, obsessions, and restlessness of the Seventies generation, he presented these traits expressively in a discourse-realm full of broken-up forces and unknowns to be explored. His works are a unique visual embodiment of youth growing up in an era of drastic reformation. In the past ten years, Yin's continually changing production has represented the self-searching and self-shaping of a generation in which idealism was instilled, but whom were deprived of their idealistic core by reality as they came of age.

著名女演员、导演，1974年生于北京，毕业于北京电影学院表演系，与章子怡、周迅、赵薇并称四大花旦。因其自导自演电影、开设网络电子杂志《开啦》及博客点击率在国内长期排名第一，故有“70后”影视圈才女之称。因其书法手写体独具个性美感，而被开发成“方正静蕾简体”字库。电影代表作有《开往春天的地铁》、《我爱你》、《将爱情进行到底》等，导演代表作有《我和爸爸》、《一个陌生女人的来信》、《杜拉拉升职记》及《亲密敌人》。

Born 1974 in Beijing, widely known actress and director, graduated from Beijing Film Institute's Performance Dept. Along with Zhang Ziyi, Zhou Xun, and Zhao Wei she has been called one of the four top camera-magnets of current cinema. Her self-directed, self-performed films, her webzine Kai-la and her blog have repeatedly been rated #1 in China, causing reporters to describe her as the female powerhouse of Chinese film. Due to unique aesthetic appeal, her calligraphy has been scanned to make the "Fangzheng Jinglei Simplifed Character Database." She has acted in noteworthy films such as *Subway to Springtime* and *I Love You*. Her representative directorial works include *Papa and I*, *Letter from an Unknown Woman*, *Du Lala's Promotion*, and *Dear Enemy*.

无法定义自我的生存体验

尹朝阳 | 徐静蕾

尹朝阳／ 我所经历的一切都比较片断，而且也很少看到一个确定的目标，因此，好像自己始终处于一种“在路上”的感觉中。包括自己的创作，很多都是并不确定的感受。

／徐静蕾 我会学习影视路上一些前辈所总结的经验，把当代的影视工作延续下来；把了解到的最当下的社会体验，通过影视真切地表现出来，用以还原这个社会的原貌。我在不断地尝试新鲜的影视理论与制作方式，用最简单、直接的形式，把心灵体验释放出来。同时，想要通过这些作品与大家产生心灵上的共鸣。

尹朝阳／ 我其实很怀疑这种生活经验的真实性，也许是因为种种新技术使用，以及过去开放三十年的积累。我们开始有某种意义上的对个人的觉醒和认识。但受制于生存环境所预设的天花板。我觉得无法定义自身的生活经验。没有任何一种东西是恒定不变的。现阶段我对几乎所有事物的印象都是暧昧的。

／徐静蕾 我从求学时期就开始尝试着通过自身的生活经验来反映一些社会现象。我觉得这一个追寻自我的过程本身就是一个还原社会、还原现代大众最真实的生活状态的方式。自己只是在不断地总结，不断地尝试，希望能用新鲜的方式反映一些所感知到的情景。70年代出生的人大多对自己的生存环境有一种不确定性的感知，在这代人出生的前几年就有了最深刻的体验。我们秉承了50、60年代人的务实主义，但同时又受到了80年代的文化冲击，所以可能需要在不断调整自己思维方式的前提下形成新的自我认知。只能在不断犯错又不断总结的基础上，逐渐形成适应社会的一套生存技能。当我迷失的时候也可能从“80后”一代的身上借鉴到一些较开放的行为方式，不断地修正自己的体验。虽然我不能解释生活经验的真实与否，但我觉得自己会认真地生活。

尹朝阳／ 也许电影艺术的表现方式，需要这样细腻的生活经验为基础。我的创作显得较为集中和纯粹，这与我自己的生存体验是平行的。

／徐静蕾 这牵扯到的是一个叙事结构的问题吧，电影与绘画还是有些区别。不过我很同意你的看法。我也是尽量从最真实的生存体验中取材，进行艺术创作，在创作中尽量体现最真实的社会体验。艺术创作算是我接触社会的皮肤，代表了最真实的我，我通过她来感知世界，体验社会。有时候我会把人生存在社会中最赤裸裸的、最具矛盾冲突的那一面叙述出来，还原一个我所体验的最真实的社会横截面。

尹朝阳／ 我觉得“70后”艺术家现在看上去，似乎都具有了某种属于个人的方向和面貌。但这也是整个艺术生态的特点。大家都在“回到常识”的路上。

/ 徐静蕾

也许是整个思维方式都在调整吧，我们都对自己的生活和艺术有了更清晰的认识。“70后”艺术家都是在肯定与否定中不断循环往复，守旧与创新中错落交织。由于“70后”沿袭着五六十年代的艺术创作思路与功底，但同时又受到“80后”新思维方式与行为模式的冲击，所以突破陈规的创作路数就成为了最极力的追求。但由于诸多时代的不确定性因素的影响与冲击，所以每隔一段时间便会产生出一个否定自己思维方式的节点，还会感觉自己本身的自我互动产生偏差，但同时也会催生出新的思维方式。

尹朝阳 /

我们毕竟到了足够感受到自己的年纪，成长起来了。或许以前情绪上不稳定的东西多一些，现在更多会理性地思考自己的想法。提到诸如“走向理性主义”，如果仅仅是种简单的“逆反”的结果，那么这种反思就基本上属于坏脾气的范围。事实上，我们缺乏真正的“理性主义”。所谓的“被确定”基本上没有太多人在乎。我只是在试图打破的同时能够见到一个新东西。

/ 徐静蕾

“70后”艺术家没有被什么标签贴上，是幸好的一种状态。我觉得这首先与“70后”的成长环境有关。在成长的最初阶段不断地接触宏大的叙述方式，浸淫在这种逻辑与思维方式中时间久了，便会想要寻求更自然更自由的表达方式来表达自己的心理状态。但在表达的同时又不希望被单一化、类型化，不希望被贴上标签，并且想用更理想的方式来叙述所体验的生活，但最难得的是要把握好这种创作的尺度，才能表达理想并浪漫。我看你的作品之中个人性的东西特别明显，你怎样理解自己的创作？

尹朝阳 /

我所有的命题都围绕个人展开。在这个善变的环境里保持一种感受的热度是必要的。现阶段艺术要解决的问题对我个人来说更像是一种手段和修炼。在消耗生命的同时可以让我看清楚自己的嘴脸。用一种看上去还贴切的手段还原出自体，并赋予它尊严，是值得的！

/ 徐静蕾

应该说，你的作品都是与自己的生命相关，而电影牵扯到更多的方面。诸如《我和爸爸》讲述了一个不谙世事的少女成长为一个少妇的心路历程，感情写得很细腻。《杜拉拉升职记》主要表达了一个初入职场的白领女孩通过自己的努力实现自己职业理想的励志故事。《将爱》可以说是通过讲述杨峥和文慧的三种感情发展路线从而引发了观众一场跨越十年的感情共鸣，这是一次更深度的情感体验。我觉得当代艺术的发展存在着与市场结合的尺度问题，这个迎合市场的尺度很难拿捏，其中有很多不可控因素在其中，只有把控好才会真实贴切地表达你所想要输出的思维方式。我始终认为艺术最重要解决的问题是结合时代的大背景忠实地表达当代人最真实的心灵体验。最基本的呈现方式就是在作品中更多地倾注自我对社会的解读，以求能够更加多元化、立体化地表达我对艺术创作的感悟。

The Existential State of the Indefinable Self

A Dialogue between Yin Chaoyang and Xu Jinglei

Yin Chaoyang / I feel that everything I have experienced has been rather fragmentary, and I have rarely had a definite aim in sight. So I always seem to have the feeling that I am "on the road." This includes my creative work: much of the time I feel it is indefinite.

Xu Jinglei / Actually I can't really claim to be a film artist. I just learn from the experiences passed on by elders in the field; in this way I carry on the work of film and video making. I take what I understand of present-day social experience and express it faithfully through film and video. I try to present the authentic face of society. I constantly experiment with fresh film theories and production methods. I use the simplest, most direct forms to release the energies of inner experience. At the same time, by means of my works I wish to strike a chord in the hearts of other people.

Yin Chaoyang / Actually I doubt that life experience can be presented with much authenticity. Maybe by use of new techniques, and with what we've built up from 30 years of open-door policies, we are starting to have some sort of awareness about individuality. But we are constrained by the ceiling that is inherent in our environment, so we are unable to define our own life experience, in my opinion. Nothing is fixed and unchanging. At the present stage my impression of practically everything is ambiguous!

Xu Jinglei / Since my student days I've been trying to use my own life experience to reflect the phenomena of society. I feel that a process of searching for oneself is, in itself, a means of recovering the most genuine things about society, about the way people live in the present day. I keep summing things up, making attempts, hoping to use fresh ways to reflect the vision I perceive. Most people born in the Seventies perceive an indefiniteness in their life environment. In the first few years after our birth we went through earth-shaking things. We embraced the pragmatism of the Fifties and Sixties generations, but at the same time we underwent the cultural impact of the Eighties. So perhaps our development of self-awareness was premised on the need for constant adjustments to our mode of thinking. Only on a foundation of repeated mistakes could we gradually build up our survival skills so we could fit into society. When I lost direction, I would absorb the example of unconstrained behavior from the Eighties generation. I kept revising my mode of being. Although I cannot explain what makes for genuineness of life experience, I am committed to approaching life seriously.

Yin Chaoyang / Perhaps the means of expression in film art needs to be based on scrutiny of life experience. My creative work seems more concentrated and pure in itself: it runs parallel to what I go through in life.

Xu Jinglei / This ties in with the question of narrative structure, I think. There are distinctions between film and painting, after all. However, I do agree with your view. I do my best to get material from the most genuine life experience, then I work with that artistically. In my creative work I endeavor to convey the most genuine social experience. Artistic creation can be considered the skin that lets me come in contact with society; it represents my most genuine self. By way of it I perceive the world and experience society. Sometimes I narrate the most jarring, conflicted side of people's social lives, to present faithfully a cross-section of society as I know it.

Yin Chaoyang / Umm-hmm. From what I can see, all Seventies generation artists seem to turn an individualistic face on the world. But this is a feature of our artistic ecology as a whole. I think everyone is on the road that leads "back to common sense."

/ Xu Jinglei

Maybe there has been an adjustment in the pattern of thinking. We are all gaining clearer recognition of our own lives and art. Artists of the Seventies generation are in a back and forth cycle between affirmation and negation, and we tend to interweave conservatism and innovation. Because our generation inherited the creative approaches and skill set of the Fifties and Sixties generation, while at the same time feeling impact from the thought and behavior patterns of the Eighties generation, they are in avid pursuit of creative moves which break through stale conventions. However, due to impact or influence from the era's numerous ambiguities, every once in a while they hit a transition point that negates their own pattern of thinking. They may even feel that their interplay of psychic tendencies is getting out of balance, but at the same time this may trigger the emergence of a new thought pattern.

Yin Chaoyang /

Yes. We have gotten to a sufficient age to get a sense of ourselves. We are starting to grow. Maybe we showed quite a bit of emotional instability in the past, but now we are more likely to take a rational approach and reflect on how our own thinking works. There are code phrases such "move toward rationality," but if it merely originates in an antagonistic stance, even reflection basically falls within the scope of bad-temperedness. Actually, we lack a true rational mentality. As for so-called "imposition of definiteness," basically there are people who don't care about it. I just try to break away from it, and meanwhile maybe see something new.

/ Xu Jinglei

The Seventies generation has not really been labeled, and I think that's a good state of affairs. I feel first of all that this relates to the environment our generation grew up in. In our earliest stage of growth we continually came in contact with the grand narrative mode. Having been immersed in this kind of logic, this mode of thinking, one wishes for a more natural, unhindered mode of expression to convey one's state of mind. Yet while expressing oneself one does not wish to be viewed from a single angle; one does not wish to be stereotyped or labeled. One wants to use relatively ideal means to narrate what one has lived through, but the tricky part is getting the sense of proportion right in your creative work, so you can express things in an ideal way, a romantic way. Looking at your works, I find their individuality is quite apparent. Tell me, how do you conceive of your creative work?

Yin Chaoyang /

All of my premises branch out from myself as an individual. In this changeable environment it's necessary to preserve some warmth of feeling. In the current phase, the problems art needs to solve, from my point of view, are choice of means and self-cultivation. While dissipating my life energy, I can see what kind of face I present to the world. Using a means that somehow fits the purpose, I present a faithful image of who I am, and I confer dignity upon it. That makes it worthwhile!

/ Xu Jinglei

I must say that your works all have to do with your own life force, but film involves many other aspects. For instance, Papa and I tells about a teen-age girl's milestones of personal growth as she grows into a young wife, with delicate descriptions of her feelings. Du Lala's Promotion is an inspirational story about a young white collar worker who achieves her professional ideals through her own efforts. Love to Come traces three threads of development in the feelings between Yang Zheng and Wen Hui: the ten-year history of their relationship yields a depth of emotional experience that strikes a chord in viewers' hearts. As for integrating contemporary art into the marketplace, I feel there is a problem of proportion. It is hard to get a handle on the extent to which one should play up to the market. There are uncontrollable factors involved in this. Only by handling them well can you successfully present the mode of thinking you want to convey. I have always felt that the most important problem art has to deal with is to convey faithfully the true inner lives of contemporary people, placing them against the overall background of the era. The most basic way to bring this about is to pour much of one's own reading of society into the work: the aim is to give it multiplicity, to convey in a layered way my insights into artistic creation.

狂热者　2011年　布面油画　250cm × 200cm

Maniac　2011　oil on canvas　250cm×200cm

狂热者　2011年　布面油画　250cm × 200cm

Maniac　2011　oil on canvas　250cm×200cm

狂热者　2011年　布面油画　285cm × 250cm

Maniac　2011　oil on canvas　285cm×250cm

狂热者　2011年　布面油画　180cm × 150cm

Maniac　2011　oil on canvas　180cm×150cm

李　晖
Li　Hui

1977年出生于北京，2003年毕业于中央美术学院，并因毕业创作《双头卡车》而广为关注。此后，李晖以其独特的观念表述方式而成为代表“观念雕塑”的重要艺术家。尤其是他以激光为媒介的作品，以绚丽但却并不稳定的视觉效应，进行一种对于社会、对于生命的自我审视，并因此而被国际当代艺术界所关注，是中国当代中能够借由并不冷涩的素材、却能探讨严肃课题的艺术家代表之一。

Born 1976 in Chongqing, graduated 2000 from Central Academy of Fine Arts, achieved fame with his graduation thesis piece *Two-Headed Trucks*. Later, owing to his uniquely concept-driven treatments, Li became a key practitioner of "conceptual sculpture." In his laser-media works, above all, he uses dazzling but unstable effects to engage in stock-taking with regards to society and living beings. For this he has attracted international notice. In contemporary China, he exemplifies artists who draw on material that is far from austere to probe serious propositions.

李 晖
Li Hui

陈小兵
Chen Xiaobing

1970年生，凯撒旅游总裁。爱好：艺术、阅读、音乐、旅游、高尔夫。

C.E.O. of Kaisa Travel Corp. His hobbies include art, reading, music, travel, golf.

纯粹指向永恒

李 晖 | 陈小兵

陈小兵／ 在这次展览的关键词中提到“晚熟”这一概念。我当时就想到在国外看到很多华人小孩，在家说中文，在外说当地的语言，可能保姆又是另外一种语言。小孩同时接触这三种语言，以至于这样的小孩在语言上似乎并不比其他只说单一语言的小孩进步快。但是在他逐渐长大之后，可能会在某一时间里突然爆发出他原有的语言积累。这跟我们“70后”的艺术家成长经历有些相似。

对，我们从小就不是只单一地接触一种状态。 ／李 晖

陈小兵／ 我是1970年的，你是文革之后出生的。你对文革有什么印象？

似乎我并不太记得什么。但是文革结束并不代表它的影响就结束，有很多遗留下来的思维方式、意识形态还会持续。你们可能更强烈，因为你们小时候的教育完全就是格式化的教育，后来才慢慢接触到多元化的社会。我理解你刚才说的例子，就是在思维方式多了之后，会突然迷失了。 ／李 晖

陈小兵／ 在同时接触到很多复杂的意识影响之后，就像小时候同时说三种语言的情况，可能不懂得用哪一种会更贴切，这个时候可能表达就会稍微慢一点，但这不代表他不理解外部的事物。

我们每个人的经历和环境都在随时变化，而且不是指一段时间是这样，以后都是这样，包括现在都在不断变化之中，我觉得“不确定”似乎是一个基调。 ／李 晖

陈小兵／ 前辈相对比较纯粹，后辈太强调自我，也很纯粹。“70后”的人却带有各种各样的元素，这种不确定性就会特别地突出。就像行走在一条道路上不断地受到各种各样的冲击，没有办法以直线延续下去，但是生命必须向前走，这个过程留下了很多痕迹。

“70后”艺术家的生存经验中，到处都是不确定的痕迹。 ／李 晖

陈小兵／ 是的，1970年代出生的人，大多都有兄弟姐妹，有时候父母对自己的影响甚至还不及兄弟姐妹。我记得那时候我们凑在一起聊天，总是爱谈哪个学校或者哪个楼里的孩子特别能打架。还有就是谁家里有几个哥哥的话，在小伙伴面前就特别自豪，因为哥哥们可以用武力来保护自己。我想这样的一种意识的形成多少是受了来自于文革时期的生存体验的影响。也就是说1970年代出生的人，到了1980年代，仍然会受到来自五六十年代的人的生存体验的影响，而且20世纪80年代也正是“70后”出生的人形成思想意识的时候。

80年代的市场经济开放之后，就出现了很多“投机倒把”的贸易者，这部分人是被瞧不起的。这其中很多都是年轻人，他们可以接受，也都是偷偷摸摸地干。我理解“不确定”，就是因为规则刚开始缓慢的变化，后来就愈演愈烈：你的价值观随时都会改变。所以，这个不确定性，绝对是和这些变化联系在一起的。我们的记忆实际上就是一些碎片，受到很多不同的价值观念的冲击，没有很长久不变的记忆。 ／李 晖

陈小兵／ 我想到崔健的一句歌词：不是我不明白，是这个世界变化快。

／李　晖 对，不过我觉得这种变化其实是自然的，因为这是生活。我也不会想到这个世界会有什么变化，因为你只能适应。回头看的话，其实身在乱中，并不觉得它乱，自己还是井井有条地做自己的事情。我觉得自己会有一种不安全感，这一点倒是有些影响。不安全感是伴随始终的，因为你不知道什么叫好。但是我们小时候所受的教育并非如此，小时候的教育它有一个好的标准。当然你的知识在逐渐积累后就慢慢会发现有些东西是错的或不全面，你会随时放弃一些东西然后往前走，在过程中适应。当然这其中你也能够找到满足感和成功，但这些东西都不能带给我们安全感。未知一定是不安全的。

陈小兵／ 这种不确定性，在1980年代社会结构发生剧变时影响了几乎所有人。这段时间正好是“70后”成长最关键的时候，这种影响对他们世界观的形成起到了很大的作用。由于生存环境的快速变化使得“70后”意识成长的整个过程都是迷失和不确定的。

／李　晖 其实这里面没有不满足，也很少有抱怨。如果你认为不对，但也改变不了现实，所以我会选择其他的方向，我觉得有很多可以选择的路。

陈小兵／ 我印象最深的就是从高中开始狂热迷恋西方摇滚乐，同学们甚至会以拥有一张美国的原版音乐录影带为荣。包括后来的港台文化，我觉得这些都一样。这些外来的文化之所以这么容易被我们接受，我觉得还是因为那个时期我们正在经历一个意识体验的真空期或者说迷失期，所以外来事物一下子就涌了进来并且很快被人们接受了。

／李　晖 阅读对我的影响，我觉得是在上大学之后。之前看武侠小说或漫画，那是青春期的选择，还有像徐克的电影。我觉得我们跟60年代的人最大的区别是，他们那个年代看的是哲学书，见面聊天也是说这些。而我们那些“发小”在那个时间段是也是聊天，但是聊的就是人生、理想、社会、政治，什么话题都聊。言外之意就是，我当时并不怎么看纸上的书。但是上大学之后有了一个模糊的方向，而且我找到一个理想的职业，有些东西确实影响了我，而且至今还有，比如说建筑的书或建筑家等。

我举个例子，就跟人的性格是相似的。一个人的性格有两面性，一个对外、一个对内，我觉得创作过程就是一个对内的过程。创作的过程，就是整个世界只有自己的存在，那是非常真实的一面。而我的创作是不着边际的事，比如我虽然不信教，但是我会读佛教的理论，去理解它的内涵，我想要是真理解出来可能对我的创作会有帮助。我的创作并不局限于什么理论，也没有别人可以指导我，我需要自己探索。这个过程就是一条特别长的路，每一个创作就是车站，这个车站可能我们能够判断出来是多远，但是我们不清楚到底要去往何处，我们只是有一个模糊的方向而已。很多人解读我的作品，指出是理性的，我可以接受，因为它不应该是感性的。我刚才所讲的例子都是感性的，我是在强调那种感觉，但不是说我的思维方式是感性的。感性是一瞬间的，与理性是交错的。

陈小兵／ 感性的东西走到一段的时候，就有理性的结晶出来。

／李　晖 真的就像你说的。比如说我今天做完一件作品，然后我会迷茫一段时间；过段时间后突然会发现我做的是什么，这需要一个过程。就是这么一点点堆积起来的，形成了一个方向。感性一段时间后，需要靠理性很长一段时间进行整理。这就是我的一个创作的过程。

陈小兵／ 我们公司的企业内刊叫《探索》，我起的名字，我觉得特别符合我们公司的情况，这可能也是中国这个时代很多企业的缩影，那就是一种探索的状态。我希望通过一个准确的名字，来告诉大家我们在做什么。你在做艺术，我在做企业，但我们的感触都很相似，我们都在探索，这里面只有过程和阶段性的成果，我们乐于在一种不确定中去寻找一种确定的东西，这也许是我们"70后"的一种宿命。

对，我们强调的都是过程，因为没有可循的模式。我也注意到"70后"的人已经在主动地进行个性表达，我觉得跟别人相同是一种耻辱。凡是宏大叙事里有的，我的作品中都不会出现。 ／李　晖

陈小兵／ 当你不知道什么是对的时候，你就无法说什么是不对的。我看过一些"70后"艺术家的作品，我觉得他们的画面表现出来一种挣扎。这种挣扎，我理解为一种探索的过程。当在探索的过程中，对自身或者外部世界不能完全确定的时候，就表现出一种挣扎的状态。

你说的1970年代艺术家的某些特点，其实都跟经历有关。还有一种可能性是，反而对变化的东西不关心了，他可能会对他认为永恒的东西感兴趣。比如空间、时间，都是永恒存在的，并不随时间的变化而变化。他就会发现有种东西是可以一直研究的，自然而然就选择了那个方向。有可能在某一时间段中，因为周围环境的影响而选择了某种东西，反而会显得很有自信，因为能够判断出来它不会变。当然这会有一个过程，因为并不是开始就有成熟的想法，而是一点点形成的。我有过很强烈的感触，作为职业画家，我们必须要做出自己的影响力。你的独特性在哪？这可以用很多种方式找到，比如视觉刺激的、看完后很安静的等，各种各样。当问题与现实发生联系的时候，便可以采取各种立场。但是，我就不会选择这种方式，因为我觉得那是一瞬间的。正因为这样，我认为自己在寻找能够一直做下去的东西。 ／李　晖

陈小兵／ 真有意思，听了你的想法之后，我对你的作品有了更深的认识。你的作品没有太多挣扎的东西，感觉是直奔主题了。也许就是刚才你说的那些永恒的东西，所以会觉得特别纯粹，看了之后能够直接到达精神层面。我在现场看你作品的时候，一瞬间就有一种进入西方教堂的体验。你作品中的光和教堂中的光给我的感受是一样的，有一种不由自主地在跟命运和上苍对话的感觉。当触碰到一些人性中永恒的东西时，可能很容易通过作品与艺术家进行意识层面的交流。

在意识到某种感觉的时候，确实有一种东西被传达出来，我就在想这是什么。这种东西是直接跟心交流的，但却是可遇不可求的。 ／李　晖

陈小兵／ 正是因为有很多的不确定，所有人都力图找到不确定中的确定，有的人是沉醉于过程，有的人是直接奔结果了。你是直接找到了这个结果，并把它表达出来了。不确定的感受是危险的，就需要找到一个确定的东西可以依赖。也正是因为有很多不确定的因素，你才可能那么执著地去寻找这个确定的东西。

我的作品就是寻找一种与人的直接沟通的方式，而不是通过一种描述来呈现。我希望观者能一眼就明白我表达的是什么，当被逼着去描述的时候，就会用语言，但是这不是他的感受。人的第一感觉肯定是喜欢与否，明白与否，不用太多的指导。当然这是我在专业上要寻找的。但是影响我的东西同样也是这个道理——不用描述的，能描述的绝对影响不了我。一些东西感觉到了就是感觉到了，我对于能够感觉到的作品会特别敏感。我也是一步一步了解自己的，了解了自己，就能真实地做作品。我们经常遇到这个问题：有了一个很成熟的想法，后来却又不做了，原因是我觉得它不应该是我做的。那么，确定不能做的原因就是，我知道自己要的是什么。 ／李　晖

Pureness Leads to Eternity

A Dialogue between Li Hui and Chen Xiaobing

Chen Xiaobing / "Late maturity" was one of the keywords mentioned about this exhibition. That reminded me of kids from Chinese families who lived abroad. They spoke Chinese at home and local languages outside, and their nannies could be speaking a third language. Though exposed to three languages, these kids do not seem to make quicker progress than those who speak only one language. When they grow up, however, their language abilities fostered over time may suddenly turn into an advantage. This is similar to the life experiences of the artists born in the 1970s.

That's right. We have been exposed to various influences since childhood. / Li Hui

Chen Xiaobing / I was born in the 1970s and you were born after the Cultural Revolution. What is your impression of the Cultural Revolution?

I don't have any clear memories of it. The ending of the Cultural Revolution did not mean that its influences vanished. Its ideological aspects and way of thinking continued to exist. Our generation may have a stronger feeling of cultural uniformity. We received a uniform, formulaic education when we were young, and we only came into contact with a pluralistic society when we grew up. I understand the example you just mentioned, but our problem is that we become lost as a result of exposure to various ideas and ways of thinking. / Li Hui

Chen Xiaobing / Being exposed to the influence of many complex ideologies is like being exposed to three languages in one's childhood. One may be slow in expressing himself because he is not sure which language is the most appropriate, but this does not mean that he is unable to understand external matters.

Our experiences and environments were, are, and will continue to be ever-changing. It seems to me that UNCERTAINTY is the underlying tone. / Li Hui

Chen Xiaobing / The older generation of artists are comparatively pure; the younger generation are more ego-centric, and they are pure in another way. Artists born in the 1970s demonstrate various elements, and, as a result, they have a stronger sense of uncertainty. One cannot walk straight and ahead down a road because he is constantly pushed about by various forces. Yet one must go on, so his journey is marked changes in direction.

The life experiences of artists born in the 1970s are laden with traces of uncertainty. / Li Hui

Chen Xiaobing / That's right. Many of those born in the 1970s have siblings. Sometimes one is more influenced by his siblings than by his parents. Many of our childhood talks focused on the strongest fighters in the school or neighborhood. One would take pride in the fact that he had quite a few elder brothers because that meant protection from his brothers. I think that such a proud feeling was influenced by life experiences of the Cultural Revolution. That is to say, even in the 1980s, those born in the 1970s were still under the influences of the life experiences of those born in the 1950s and 1960s. The 1980s were the period for the mental and psychological development of those born in the 1970s.

When China began to develop its market economy in the 1980s, many traders appeared. People looked down on them as "opportunists and brokers." Many of them were young people and they did their business underground. There was uncertainty because the rules were changed gradually at first and then drastically, and your values were changed as a result. Therefore I would say that uncertainty is related to changes. In fact, my memories are fragmentary; they are subject to the impacts of different values. There is no such a thing as permanent, unchanging memory. / Li Hui

Chen Xiaobing / This reminds me of the lyrics by Cui Jian: It's not that I don't understand, but the world is changing too fast.

/ Li Hui

That's right, but I think such changes are unavoidable. They are part of our life. I do not anticipate us making great changes in this world, because we can only adapt ourselves to the world. Looking back, I don't think I was confused in a world of confusion; I have been working in an orderly manner. I think I feel a sense of insecurity, and this has an impact on me. The feeling of insecurity is always there because you don't know what is good. Yet this was not the case with our early education where there were standards for what was good. Yet as you learn more, you gradually realize that what used to be right turns out to be wrong or incompletel. Then you give up some things from time to time and keep moving forward; you adapt yourself in this process. You can certainly achieve successes or gratifications, but these do not bring a sense of security. The unknown is definitely unsafe.

Chen Xiaobing / Such uncertainty had an impact on almost everyone in the 1980s when great changes took place in our social structures. That was also the crucial period for the coming of age of those born in the 1970s, and it certainly played an important role in shaping their outlooks. Their coming of age was characterized by confusion and uncertainty because of rapid changes in their living environments.

/ Li Hui

In fact, one did not feel a lot of dissatisfaction or resentment as all this went on. You could not change reality even though you thought it was wrong. So you turned to other options, and trusted that other routes would open up.

Chen Xiaobing / What I remember most clearly is that we became rock and roll fans starting in middle school, and having an original American music video would make one a hero among his schoolmates. Later, we became fans of Hong Kong and Taiwan cultures. I think it was a time of being lost, when we were experiencing a vacuum, so foreign cultures found their way into China easily and were immediately accepted.

/ Li Hui

Reading began to have an impact me only after college. I also read martial arts novels and cartoon books and watched movies by Xu Ke. Those were the choices of our adolescent days. A big difference between us and those born in the 1960s is that they read and talked about philosophy. I would also chat a lot with my childhood friends, but we mostly talked about life, ambitions, society, politics, and many other topics. That means we did not read many printed books. After college I had a vague idea of where I wanted to go and got myself a job I loved. Some people and things had an influence on me, and they still influence me today, for example architects and architecture books.

Let me use a man's personality as an example. A man's personality has an outward and an inward side. I think creative work is an inward process, where there is the existence of only one person in the entire world and where one faces his true self. My creative work is a boundless process. I am not a Buddhist, but I read Buddhist theories and try to understand them, because I think that thorough understanding of Buddhist ideas may help with my art production. I don't follow any given theory, nor can anyone guide me through my art production process. I need to find my own way. This process is a long road, and each work produced marks a station on that road. I can figure out the distances between stations, but cannot tell where the road leads to. What I have is only a general direction. Many people say that my works are rational, and I agree with that, because I don't want works of sensibility. The examples I just provided are have strong sensibility. I emphasize feeling, but it does not mean that my way of thinking is sensibility-based. Sensibility happens in the blink of an eye, and it is interlaced with reason.

Chen Xiaobing / Sensibility will produce rational crystals at certain points.

You are absolutely right. After a work is finished, I will feel perplexed for some time before I suddenly realize what I have created. This process takes time. Things accumulate over time and then there is a direction ahead of you. I usually need a long time to rationalize my perceptions accumulated over time, and this is my art creation process. / Li Hui

Chen Xiaobing / My company runs an internal journal called Exploration. This title, which I gave to the journal, describes exactly how the company is run, and it also represents the state of many Chinese enterprises: they are all doing exploration. I wanted to use this title to tell people what we were doing. You create art, while I run an enterprise, but we have similar experiences because we are both doing exploration, and this involves periodic achievements. We would like to find certainty in the uncertain. Maybe this is the destiny of as members of the Seventies generation.

Yes, we all agree that it is a process because there is no established model we can follow. I have also noticed that those born in the Seventies are actively committed to personal expression. I think being identical with others is humiliating. Whatever exists in the grand narrative does not appear in our works. / Li Hui

Chen Xiaobing / When you are not sure what is right, you cannot tell what is wrong. I have seen some works by artists born in the 1970s, and I can see a kind of struggle in their paintings. I think such struggle is a process of exploration. In this process, one is in a state of struggling when he is not completely sure of himself or the outside world.

Some attributes of the artists born in the 1970s are related their experiences. Another possibility is that they no longer care about change but are interested in what they think of as eternal, such as time and space, which are eternal and do not change with time. They find something in which they can continuously invest their exploratory efforts and they progress in that direction. There may come a time when one makes a choice under the influence of his environment, yet does so with a fair degree of confidence that what he has chosen will be enduringly valid. This certainly takes time; a mature idea is formed over time. I feel strongly that, as professional painters, we must create our own influences. What makes one different from the others? There are various approaches. For example, your paintings can be visually shocking in a way that gives the viewer a cathartic release. When connections are built between an issue and the reality, we can choose sides. Yet I would not opt for this approach because I think it is transient. This is the reason why I am looking for something I can work on for the long term. / Li Hui

Chen Xiaobing / This is very interesting. What you just said has increased my understanding of your paintings. It seems to me that there isn't much struggle in your paintings, you go straight ahead toward the main point. Perhaps this is the eternal thing that you just mentioned. It is quite pure, and I can arrive at its spiritual level by simply looking at it. The moment I stand before your paintings, I seem to be entering a church. To me, the light in your works is the same as the light in a church, and I seem to be having a dialogue with Destiny and Heaven. When we touch on the eternal parts of man's nature, it is easy for us to have consciousness-level communication with the artist through his art.

When you are aware of the existence of certain feelings, something is communicated through art. I've been trying to figure out what it is. Such heart-to-heart communication happens only by chance. / Li Hui

Chen Xiaobing / Many people try to find certainty in the uncertain precisely because there are so many uncertain things. Some people enjoy the process while others just head for the result. You arrived at the result directly and have expressed it. The feeling of uncertainty is threatening, so one must find some thing certain to rely on. You doggedly look for such a thing as certainty precisely because there are so many uncertain factors everywhere.

Li Hui / In my paintings I look for an approach for direct communication with others rather than presenting such communication through descriptions. I hope the audience will be able to understand what I intend to show. Language is used when one is forced to describe something, but this is not his feelings. One's immediate feeling is whether he likes something or not, understands it or not. Guidance is unnecessary here although it is what I need for my professional career. This is also the case with what has influenced me: it must be something indescribable. What is describable will never have an influence me. Some things can be understood, and I am particularly sensitive towards works I can understand. I have come to understand myself gradually, and I can create true works when I understand myself. Sometimes I get a mature idea but later find myself unable to actualize it because I don't think this is what I should do. This is an issue we frequently encounter. The reason I determine it is not for me, then, is that I know what I need.

V　激光灯，镜子，烟雾　2011年　可变尺寸，依据现场而定

V　Laser, Mirror,Smog　2011　Variable Dimensions, according to the space

琥珀　2006年　亚克力板，LED灯，不锈钢　240cm × 120cm × 60cm

Amber　2006　Acrylics, LED Lamp, Stainless Steel　240cm×120cm×60cm

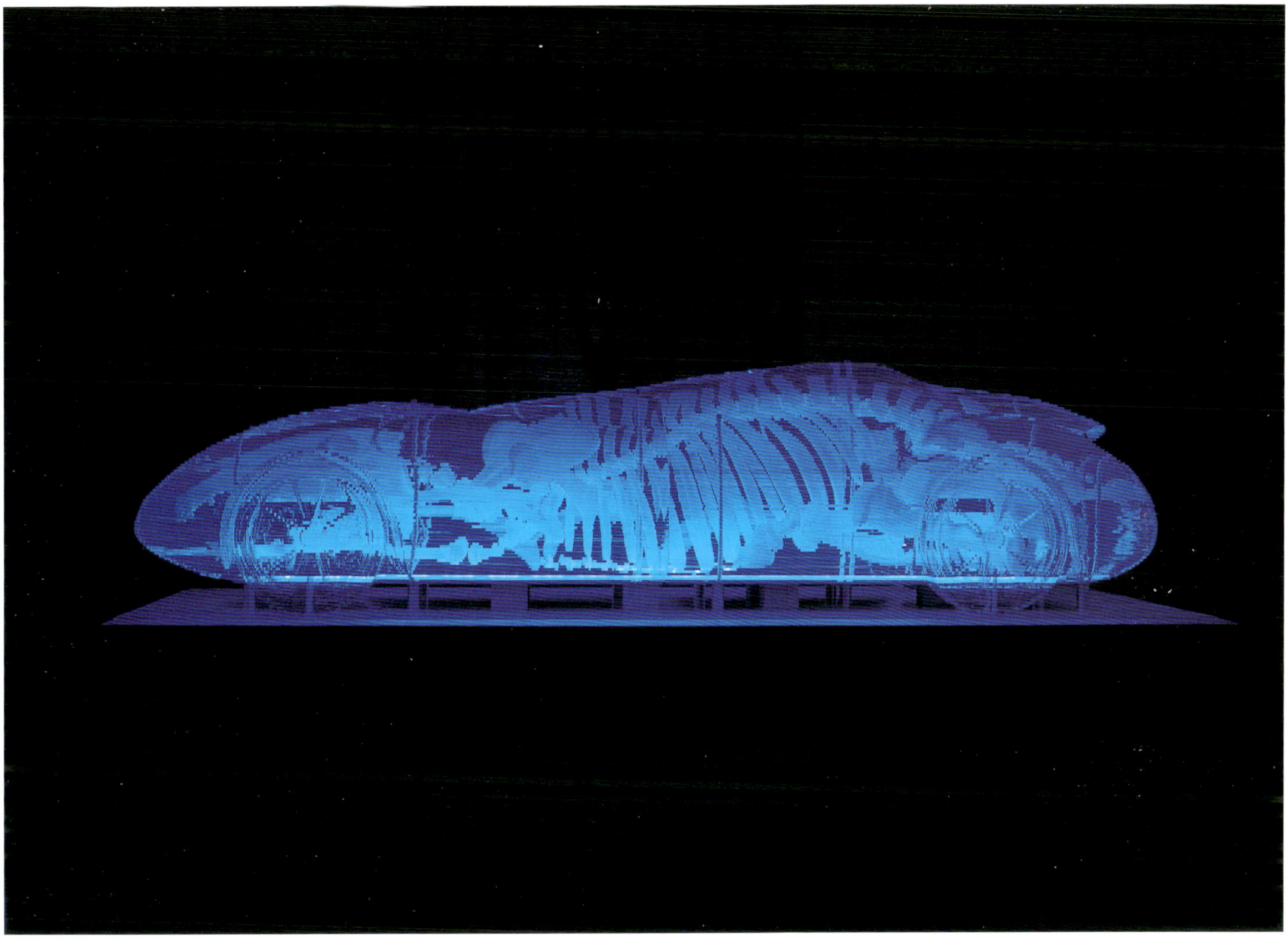

蜕变　2006年　不锈钢，木头　450cm × 220cm × 80cm

Metamorphosis　2006　Stainless Steel, Wood　450cm×220cm×80cm

贪心不足　2011年　铝塑板，不锈钢　450cm × 250cm × 200cm

Greed　2011　Aluminum plastic board, Stainless Steel　450cm×250cm×200cm

李继开
Li Jikai

1975年生于成都。2004年毕业于四川美术学院油画系，获硕士学位。在“70后”绘画中，“卡通题材”是无法回避的话题之一。虽然，大多这种流行样式的作品趋于简单化、概念化，以至丧失了精神表达的价值，但李继开无疑是个例外。他沉浸于个人想象的世界中，将一个具有童年色彩的白日梦描绘得沉郁而自足，具有一种孤寂的冥想感。从某种角度看，他的这种内向反省式的图像经验，正是“70后”理想主义教育面对外在现实无处依托，转而自我构建的形象呈现。

Born 1975 in Chengdu, graduated 2004 with M.F.A. from Oil Painting Dept., Sichuan Fine Arts Institute. Among Seventies generation paintings, "cartoon subject matter" is an unavoidable topic. Although works with popular motifs tend to be simplified and concept-heavy, to the point that spiritual values are not expressed at all, Li is clearly an exception to this tendency. Immersing himself in a personal imaginative world, he depicts child-like daydreams that are somber and complete unto themselves,with a solitary meditative feel. In a sense, his inwardly reflective imagery is an emblem of the Seventies generation: having confronted the external world and found nothing to support the ideals instilled in them, they turn their energies toward self-edification.

李继开
Li Jikai

李芊润
Li Qianrun

《大周末hotspot》执行出版人兼执行主编，资深媒体人、策划人。2007年组织创办大型城市时尚文化周刊《大周末hotspot》，开创国内时尚文化原创周刊先河，在视觉表达以及文化艺术与时尚相互介入等领域大胆尝试突破，弘扬原创精神与生命力，形成独树一帜的刊物风格和强大的城市影响力。近年组织策划多项大型公众城市文化活动与展览，引起强烈反响，成功探索出城市时尚文化周刊在城市文化中新的存在方式。

Executive magazine publisher, veteran media figure, curator. In 2007 she founded the fashion-culture weekly *Dazhoumo hotspot*, breaking new ground in China's publishing scene with overlapping coverage of two fields. She has staged eye-popping mutual interventions between art/culture and fashion, upholding the spirit of originality and love of life. She has created a unique fashion periodical style with the power to influence urban culture. In recent years she has put on large urban culture events that have been highly acclaimed by the public. She has pioneered a new role for her cultural weekly as an indispensable part of the urban cultural mix.

天真而困惑的内在世界

李继开 丨 李芊润

李继开／ 从小到大，无非就是读书上学。我生于1975年，父亲是老师，母亲是个医生。我很小就喜欢画画，后来小学时画了很短时间的水墨画，其他时间在课本里乱画。更多的时间是一个人画和玩，在课本上画，在墙上画。现在回想起来，小孩子是最容易自我满足的，可以通过各种方法去营造一个自己可以相信的世界。而画画其实只是玩的一部分，占用我的时间也并不多。有时回忆这些，已经一时记不起很多生活的细节，只是知道物质条件慢慢在丰富，周围的人也很具体地越来越忙。时间会改变一切，一切在这些过程中的种种经历感受，会自然地在过程中被磨平洗去。因为人总是会把自己看得太重，所以会有痛苦，所以会有对他人的喜爱和怨恨。每个人的起点与终点都是相同的，各种快乐与痛苦，希望与失落，就像四季轮回一样让人新鲜地去习惯着，时间过得太快了，时常觉得我们是多么不了解他人，也不了解自己。

／李芊润 我也经常有这种时间的错愕感，尤其是回想自己的经历时。作为70年代初出生的人，我的童年甚至刚刚进入少年的那个时期还是有相当长的一段是在一种表面很平静的，就像电影《阳光灿烂的日子》那样有很多安静和耀眼的正午的那样的氛围下成长过来的。整个社会物质比现在匮乏很多，人们对物质的要求也相对朴素。那个时候视野也的确比较窄，看的国外的书也都是什么《简·爱》、《福尔摩斯》、《呼啸山庄》那些个时期的作品，大多数人甚至并不知道真正发达和先进的国家意味着什么，所以当时包括80年代的时候走出国门的人一到美国去一看就傻了。这是一种巨大的视野上的真空和脱节，这种脱节导致的观念等方方面面的对于人的冲击，是“90后”尤其是“00后”恐怕难以想象的。我特别想了解你的绘画经历是怎样的，为什么会呈现出孤独和忧郁的情绪？

李继开／ 是这样吗？一晃我已经画了很多年了，但还是年轻人。还记得大学一年级时回家里都在破沙发上画画的情景，人很单纯，还有第一次一个人租的房子，对着漆黑的夜画夜景。又像写生又像闭门造车的瞎画。想起90年代初期粗糙朴素的情感与生活。那无知随便的考生时代，那自以为是的求学时代，一切都已过去了。那只是个自然的过程。很个人化的东西我想不用刻意去隐藏，人都知道如何对待自己，对待生活，就像饿了要吃，困了要睡一样。在我成长和生活的年代，到现在我仍能想起小时候各个阶段被“艺术”打动的人或事，有来自于图像的，有来自于故事的，也有来自于自己从事绘画过程所经历的。想必你也体验过这种情绪吧？

／李芊润 进入80年代之后，我很明显地感觉到，自己被裹挟进一种被变革的生存状态，完整经历了这30年来让全世界都震惊的中国社会一波一波的巨大变革，自己对于社会、对于人的各种价值观和判断不断地被挑战。身为“70后”，我对于所生存的时代似乎始终没有可以自然而然跟随的这种归属感，而是充满带有明显不确定性的、有些尴尬的、怀疑的这种生存体验。这种不断被冲击的现实经历其实从客观上来讲也成为了一种训练，形成了一种对社会的冷观的视角。有些人认为你的作品中存在一种天真的想象，你是怎样看的？

李继开／ 每个人都会有天真的一面，只不过很多时候是保留给了家人，或是最亲密的人。这种纯真是生活得以继续的很重要的一部分，来自天真的、困惑的内在世界，是一个很个人化的事情。艺术创作是感受、体验的某种外延。现在觉得生活本身和对生命和存在的感悟比艺术（或者这工作，这行业）更重要，一个人自信自爱的干点事情就好，可以随意地去认真干事情。学会去慢慢发现和承认自己。就如同一件作品的开始，和慢慢成型，都有自己成长的逻辑。慢慢很多东西会被自然地放弃或确立。人对事物的过分追求是一种荒唐，对某些人、某些事、某些物都是如此。除了日常生活外，绘画就是确立自己对人生和对自己的一种态度，有足够的时间可以怀疑自己和生活。老之将至，这件事情实在是太严肃了，有时候回忆过去，那些事情是怎样慢慢发生变化的，变化得让人察觉不到，而到了发现的那天，发现这不过是人世间的普遍规律而已。一代人来，一代人去，太阳照常升起。人本质上也许就是自己面对自己一个人的终极现实。随着年龄增长，我开始慢慢变成一个迷信的人了。

我与你的很多感受是非常相似的。的确，“70后”的这批人骨子里挺纯真的，是比较理想主义的一批人，这其实挺不可思议的，经历了这么多大的变革。在颠覆中成长起来的“70后”，是在对社会的旁观和对自身的不断审视和迷失中走过来的，一方面我们特别愿意与这个世界交流，一方面孤独成了我们喘息的，甚至是对抗社会的一种方式。各种不确定性告诉我们没有什么是可以依赖和凭借的，我们习惯抽离，却不得不紧盯着社会的风吹草动。这反而让我们做事情没那么容易局限或者过于个人化，具体到做事情往往还是愿意去做一些创新性的、比较大的题材的、有社会性、有反思意味的事情。你觉得有什么关键词，适合描述“70后”艺术家的精神内核？ ／李芊润

李继开／ 我想不出有什么关键词来概括“70后”艺术家群体，太阳底下无新事，事情刚开始的时候，总是美好的。艺术不应该是有标准答案的。直觉很重要，对某种趣味的疏离或亲近。如同一个人一生的自然成长一样，创作中某种动力或者态度，往往就是自觉作用。直觉就是说你以为自己没有思想，但其实是有的，但懒得去说清楚它。老去认识自己很累的。还是洗东西比较好，一切像都又重新开始了一样。不知道你怎样看？

“70后”是比“50后”和“60后”现实，比“80后”和“90后”理想主义的一个群体。我们内心深处还是认同人是应该活得有价值，为了理想所做的是最有价值的等等这些很传统的观点；但是我们又不断地被现实的光鲜亮丽的诱惑所强烈地干扰，羡慕“80后”、“90后”那种可以及时行乐地放下包袱的轻松感，尝试他们不去主动背负太多的这种比较开放的生存方式。这种反差促使我们喜欢不断去打破，去推翻之后再重新创造。 ／李芊润

李继开 / 我觉得打破之后，未必就能建构一个更好的东西。我会选择很诚实地面对自己的过去，就会发现自己和自己小时候其实并无多大分别。一个人所拥有的资源就决定了他成为什么样子的人，艺术也是如此。时代对个人的影响一定是大的，对我来说日子一天天过去，人在一天天成长，经历一些事情，结识一些人，彼此都在这个时空里一天天长大变老，感受到自己和世界越来越热闹，新鲜又盲目。绘画无论对一个小孩子还是对成年的我来说，都是一件容易而又困难的事情。这个事情有点像宗教，你要信它，认真对它，觉得这个地方搞一搞会很有意思，那出来的结果自己就会满意。如果一个人心都乱了，有再好的条件，再好的方法，都没用的。它没有一个诱惑在那里了。我想这可能是纯手工创作都需要具备的一种感受。这一百年来世界发展太快，我仍记得儿时父母在生活里的惜物之情，通过手和劳作，表达内心。我以为自己和别人并无不同，个人精神世界的描述要达到准确，我可能也没有这个能力。语言越准确，也许歧义就会越大，每个人的表达都是个人化表达，只是形式不同而已。就像生活一样，无谓正道歧途，不要把自己生活弄糟就好。虽然从生存体验而言有很多不确定性的因素，然而我还是倾向于冷静面对自己的生活。

/ 李芊润 这应该就是一种非常理性的生活和工作态度。我总体验到，这种理性主义的反思存在于“70后”的骨子里，是整个生长和生存的历程决定的。它的确有它的价值，但同时也确实常常会让人感觉很累，或者说不太可爱。其实“不确定性”是好玩儿的，是会带给你创作生命力的东西。而在当下，反思宏大叙事的同时，我相信很多“70后”和我一样也在不断反思理性主义在当下该呈现出的尺度和方式，怎样能够合时宜地、更浪漫地、更生活化地、甚至更轻松地表达价值，这其实是需要不断去摸索的。就像我们搞的一些大型的公众时尚文化活动，形式很轻松、很时尚，甚至很诙谐，但是它是架构在理性的思考之上的。再好比姜文的《让子弹飞》，“不确定”成了他思考的方式。

李继开 / 我倾向于一种自由和感触性的绘画思路。绘画分解开来，也就是一些颜料、刷子在画布上的运动，留下的痕迹，不停地组合排列，轻重缓急。过程感受是最重要的。看看想想，有没有达到自己的意愿，通过一次次的观看，也会明白自己能否容忍这种趣味。对于绘画而言，结果总是虚无的。一张画结束了、开始了，有什么关系，一切仍是遥不可及，一切都比不上生活本身更直接。在描绘中感受自信和自我警惕，失落与怀疑。绘画作为一种手工劳作，技术性成分一定是有的，手感在抽象的笔触颜色感觉里是无法抽离分析的。隐晦的个性通过绘画反映在方方面面。艺术创作可以使作者拥有两个人生，现实的和虚构的。画中物与人和我的关系，是某时某刻因为某个兴趣去画了它们，它们不代表我一直以来在思考什么，但一定和我的生活状态有关。有条理、有步骤地去分析自己，我认为这是不靠谱的事情。我爱观察周围的人，度过有意思和没意思的一天又一天。不知道你作为一个媒体人，是怎样理解艺术与生活的关系的？

我们《大周末hotspot》团队从创刊开始就一直在做和艺术有关的一些推动工作，包括策划大型的公众时尚文化活动，像今年的“我爱×××”和“城市趣味：明星名人当代艺术推荐收藏展”等等，一直都从一个城市刊物的视角在探索将城市中各种时尚与文化的力量整合起来，推动形成更好的城市精神层面的时尚文化局面，构建当下城市更好的趣味。艺术在我看来它还是在反映人的生存状态和人的思考的，我们这么做其实也是希望当代艺术能够在自身突破的同时能够带动更多的人群，能够在人们的生活中实现它更丰富的价值。

/李芊润

An Inner World of Innocence and Perplexity

A Dialogue between Li Jikai and Li Qianrun

Li Jikai / From childhood to adulthood I've always been going to school. I was born in 1975; my father was a teacher and my mother was a doctor. From a very young age I liked drawing pictures; later in primary school I practiced ink painting for a little while. The rest of the time I was drawing this or that in my textbooks. Most of the time I drew all alone for fun: I drew in textbooks, I drew on walls. Looking back, I think a child can find contentment pretty easily; by various means he can make a world that he can believe in. Actually, drawing pictures was only one form of play and it did not take up a large portion of my time. Sometimes when I think back on these things, I cannot recall many details of the past, but I do recall that material conditions slowly got more prosperous, and the people around me became increasingly busy, in very concrete ways. Time can change everything: as time passes, all sorts of experiences are rubbed flat and washed away. Because people tend to overvalue themselves, one may end up suffering pain; one may develop fondness or resentment towards other people. Each person's starting point and end point are similar. All the varieties of pain and delight, hope and discouragement go around like the cycle of seasons, bringing people fresh things to get used to. Time passes too quickly. I often get a feeling that we don't understand other people very well; we don't even understand ourselves.

Li Qianrun / I also often feel startled by the passage of time, especially when I think back on my own experiences. As a person born early in the Seventies, my childhood and initial phase of adolescence went by in a period that was calm on the surface, like the tranquil, dazzling midday in the film In the Heat of the Sun … Society as a whole was lacking in material things compared to now, and people were relatively modest in their demand for possessions. Back then our horizons were indeed fairly narrow. What few foreign books we read—such as Jane Eyre, Sherlock Holmes, and Wuthering Heights—were all from an earlier period. Most people had no idea what things were like in truly developed, advanced countries. So those who went out into the world at that time, and in the Eighties, were dumbfounded by what they saw in America. The big holes in their world view caused a huge dissonance, and the impact of this dissonance, conceptually and otherwise, is probably hard for the Eighties generation and especially the Nineties generation to imagine. I am especially interested in what your experience has been as a painter. Why does your work convey a mood of solitude and melancholy?

Li Jikai / Is that how it strikes you? In a flash all these years of painting have gone by, but I'm still a young person. I still remember my freshman year of college when I would return home and sit painting on a worn-out sofa. I didn't want anything more. I still remember the first room I rented, how I gazed into the darkness and painted night scenes. I painted as I saw fit, sometimes painting from life but sometimes closing myself off from all influence. I recall my crude, plain emotions and way of life in the early Nineties. I remember my unknowing, casual period of exam-preparation, and my know-it-all period as a student. It is all receding into the past now: that is just a natural process. There are some quite personal things, but I don't make a point of concealing them. Each person knows how to deal with himself, how to deal with life, for instance when you're hungry you eat and when you're tired you sleep. Looking back on the period when I grew up and tasted life, I can recall people and incidents from each youthful phase when I was moved by "art." Some of the feelings came from pictures I saw, some from stories I heard, and some came from my own experiences in the process of painting. I think you also must have gotten a taste of such emotions.

Li Qianrun / When the Eighties rolled around, I clearly felt that I was caught up in a situation of drastic reform. I went through each wave of the massive 30-year reforms in China—a process that the world viewed with amazement. My value judgments about reality and about people were constantly being challenged. As a member of the Seventies generation I never felt a sense of belonging to something that I could follow naturally. Instead, my sense of existence was filled with indefiniteness, awkwardness and doubt. This real-life experience of continuous impacts, in objective terms, amounted to a kind of training, letting me develop a dispassionate perspective on society.

Some people see an innocent imaginative power in your works. What do you think of this?

Li Jikai /

Every person has an innocent side, but in many cases it is reserved for one's family or the persons one feels close to. This kind of purity is important for life's continuance. What you make of that inner world of innocence and perplexity is a highly individual matter. Artistic creation is an externalization of feeling, of your sense of being alive. Now I feel that living and insight into existence are more important than art. (I mean the occupation, the line of work.) If a person turns his hand to something with confidence and self-esteem, then that is enough: you can turn your hand to anything, just as you wish. Learning to discover yourself and acknowledge yourself, over time, is like beginning an artwork and seeing it take shape over time: in both cases there is an inherent logic of growth. Over time some things will be gotten rid of, and some things will be reaffirmed. Absurdity results when a person pursues something excessively, whether a person, an outcome or a physical thing. Aside from what one deals with in daily life, painting reaffirms a certain attitude toward one's life and toward oneself: it means that one takes the time to call oneself and one's life into question. As old age draws near, this becomes a serious matter. Sometimes I recall how things in the past changed: the change they underwent happened over time, in a way that you couldn't detect, and then the day would come when you would discover it, and you would discover that this was just an ordinary principle of the human world. A generation comes and a generation goes, but the sun keeps rising as always. In essence the ultimate reality for a person is that he confronts himself alone. With increasing age, I am gradually becoming a superstitious person.

/ Li Qianrun

Many of my perceptions are quite similar to yours. Indeed, these Seventies artists are a bunch of pure people if you look deep down. This is a fairly idealistic bunch of people, which is really pretty inconceivable, considering what huge historical shifts they've been through. This generation grew up in a context that was being subverted: they came through a phase of being onlookers of society, of continually taking stock of themselves and sometimes losing their way. On one hand we are willing to engage in give and take with this world, but on the other hand, solitude has become the air we breathe, and has even become a means of resisting society. Various forms of indefiniteness tell us that there is nothing we can depend on, no ultimate ground. We are in the habit of detaching ourselves, yet we have no choice but to watch every little ripple in the currents of social change. But this is good, because in our work we cannot easily go off into our own little corners of individuality. In our concrete work we are often willing to take on innovative projects, covering large subjects, with social relevance and reflective significance.

What sort of key words do you think would fittingly describe the core spirit of Seventies generation artists?

Li Jikai /

I can't think of any key words to encapsulate Seventies generation artists in the aggregate. There is nothing new under the sun. When things are first beginning, that is when they are most beautiful. Art should not have a standard answer. Intuition is important when drawing near to or distancing yourself from a certain taste. Just like a person's natural growth during his lifetime, the driving force or attitude in creative work is often self-awareness. If intuition is at work, you yourself may suppose that you have no ideas, but actually you do: it's just that you can't be bothered to state them in so many words. Always trying to be aware of oneself can be tiring. It's better to wash things clean, so it's as if you're starting everything afresh. I wonder what your view of this is.

/ Li Qianrun

The Seventies generation is post-realist relative to the Fifties and Sixties generations. Compared to the post-idealist Eighties and Nineties generations, we have an inner conviction that people should live for certain values, that what is done for the sake of ideals has great value, and all those other traditional concepts. But we are continually being disrupted by lurid temptations of reality. I envy the relaxed attitude of the Eighties and Nineties generations that lets them put down their burdens and seize the moment. I'd like to try their relatively hedonistic style that is not encumbered by a sense of mission. Due to contrasting tendencies, we like to smash and overturn things, but afterward we like to create something all over again.

Li Jikai /

I feel that once you smash things, you may not be able to construct anything better. My choice is to confront my own past, in all sincerity, and in doing so I discover there's no great distinction between myself now and when I was little. The resources at a person's disposal decide what kind a person he'll turn into, and that is true of an artist too. Our era is bound to have a huge influence on a person. As for me, the days go by, and every day I am growing. I am going through certain events, getting to know certain people, and we witness each other growing older, day by day, in this setting. I feel that I am getting caught up, along with the world, in more and more commotion, ever fresh but without direction. Whether in the eyes of a child or an adult like me, painting is an easy thing to do, but at the same time it's difficult. It is a little bit like religion: you have to believe in it, to treat it seriously, and you feel it would be intriguing to put some time into this or that aspect, so you can come up with a result that satisfies you. If a person's mind is all in a mess, it doesn't matter how good conditions are for him, or how good of a method he uses use, it will be all for nothing. There has to be something luring you onward or it won't work. I think there probably has to be this kind of feeling in any kind of creative work that depends on craftsmanship. In this past century the world has been developing too fast. I still remember how my parents cherished things in the course of daily life, and how they conveyed what was in their hearts by work of their hands. I really don't consider myself different from other people. If one is expected to achieve exactitude in depicting one's own spiritual world, I probably lack such ability. The more exact language becomes, the more divergences there will probably be. Each person's expression will be individualized, but that will only be a formal difference. It's the same as in life—there is no such thing as a proper path or a bypath, as long as you don't turn your life into a mess. Although life brings us up against many indefinite factors, I favor keeping a clear head as I face life.

/ Li Qianrun

That sounds like quite a rational attitude toward life and work. This kind of rational reflection goes deep down in the bones of the Seventies generation: it is determined by the whole environment we grow and survive in. Rationality has value for us, but at the same time it can be taxing, or perhaps even tiresome. Actually, indefiniteness is fun: it can bring creativity alive. At present, even while they are reflecting on grand narratives, I believe that many members of the Seventies generation, like me, are reflecting on the scale and mode that rationality ought to have in the present context. How can it be in tune with the times; how can it be more romantic, more concerned with daily life, or even more easygoing in its way of addressing values? To find out, we have to keep feeling our way along. For instance, we have put on large-scale fashion and culture events for the public. The form is easygoing, keyed into fashion, even humorous, but it is built on rational considerations. Another example is Jiang Wen's Let Bullets Fly: in that movie indefiniteness becomes his prime mode of thinking.

Li Jikai /

The path I tend to follow in painting is one of free responses to what touches me. If you break painting down to its elements, it is just pigments, brushes and movements across canvas; these movements leave marks, which you continually combine and rearrange, making adjustments in proportion and emphasis. Your perception of the process is the important thing. You look at how it turns out and consider whether or not you achieved what you had wished. By looking repeatedly, you determine whether or not this is agreeable to your taste. With respect to the act of painting, the result is invariably empty. You finish one piece, then go on to the next—it does not seem to matter; what you're doing seems out of touch; none of it can compare with the directness of life itself. But amidst these depictions, you feel confidence or wariness about what you're doing. As a kind of craftsmanship, painting definitely has technical elements. Your active tactile experience cannot be abstracted from the impression given by your brushwork and color; your hidden personality is reflected in many visible aspects of the painting. Artistic effort can allow the creative worker to have two lives: one in reality and one as a fictive construct; relations with fellow humans on one hand and, and objects in a painting on the other. You painted them because something caught your interest at such and such a moment, but they don't represent what you've been pondering over a long period of time. Yet they surely have some relation to your state of being. I feel that to analyze oneself methodically is a dicey matter. I love to observe people around me. I watch the days go by, some of them more interesting than others. How about you? As a media person, how do you view the relation of art and life?

/ Li Qianrun

I've always felt that a media outlet which possesses a truly urban spirit has a responsibility to do promotions that are related to art, and that includes producing large-scale fashion and culture events for the public. This year we've put on at least two of them: "I Love XXX" and "Urban Tasted: Celebrity-Endorsed Contemporary Art Expo." From the perspective of an urban journal, we've been exploring how to integrate various forces of fashion and culture in our city, to push for a fashion-plus-culture scene that can better embody our urban spirit. We are providing conditions for enhancement of taste in our city. I view at as reflecting people's state of being and their thinking. In fact we hold these events in hope that art, while making its own breakthroughs, can stimulate a wider spectrum of people, so its values can be realized more richly in people's lives.

少年面孔　2011年　布面丙烯　50cm × 40cm

Juvenile's Face　2011　acrylic on canvas　50cm×40cm

废墟里点火的男孩　2011年　布面丙烯　160cm × 230cm

Sparking in the Ruins　2011　acrylic on canvas　160cm×230cm

灯笼　2011年　布面丙烯　145cm × 200cm

Lantern　2011　acrylic on canvas　145cm×200cm

蘑菇与男孩　2011年　布面丙烯　200cm × 150cm

Mushroom and the Boy　2011　acrylic on canvas　200cm×150cm

屠宏涛
Tu Hongtao

1976年生于四川成都，1999年毕业于中国美院油画系。在“70后”艺术家中，屠洪涛的作品弥漫着某种迷茫、困惑的情绪特征。其作品多为场景相对混乱的人群、楼群或舞台，在并不强调主题的状态下，表达出我们生存世界的某种“无所适从”的精神体验。与此种体验相关的，是他充满质感的语言与笔触，在流动的绘画性中显现出绘画自身的感受方式。

Born 1976 in Chengdu, Sichuan, graduated 1999 from Oil Painting Dept., China Academy of Art. Among Seventies generation artists, Tu's works are notable for a pervasive mood of anomie and perplexity. His works present disordered scenes of crowds, housing developments, stage sets. Through de-emphasis of theme, he conveys the aimlessness our spirits undergo in the current realm of survival. His language and brushwork are full of texture. With their fluid painterly values, his works manifest a mode of painting that is native to painting.

屠宏涛
Tu Hongtao

尹丽川
Yin Lichuan

自由作家、诗人，1973年生于重庆，毕业于北京大学西方语言文学系及法国ESEC电影学校。出版过小说诗歌合集《再舒服一些》、长篇小说《贱人》，作品发表于《天涯》、《芙蓉》、《现场》、《北京文学》等，为1970年代作家中的代表人物。2006年执导电影处女作《公园》，之后的《牛郎织女》曾参加戛纳电影节“导演双周”竞赛单元，新作《与时尚同居》也受到了社会各界的关注。

Born 1972 in Chongqing, free-lance writer and poet, graduated from Beijing University, Foreign Languages Dept. and ESEC Film School, France. Has published a poetry collection, *Make It Feel Better* and the full-length novel *Lowlife*. He works have appeared in *Tianya*, *Furong*, *Xianchang*, and *Beijing Literature*. She is a representative writer of the Seventies generation. . In 2006 she directed her first film, *Park*. Her film *Herdboy and Weaver Maid* took part in the "Directors Biweekly" event at Cannes. Her new film *Cohabiting with Fashion* has been well received in film and fashion circles.

理性主义在于回归生命的常态

屠宏涛 | 尹丽川

屠宏涛／ 提到文化大革命，应该与我没有什么直接的关系了。从小的生活一直很普通，但我也感觉到幸福。1991 年去重庆后开始独立生活，感受到很多书本里学不到的东西。记得那时人很喜欢打架，喝酒。学校中没有电视但有了游戏机。吃粮票、饭票。如果喜欢一个女生，要学习新的香港流行歌曲，而读诗歌开始过时啦。1995年到了杭州学习，学校里还没有太大的贫富差别，主要聊天的内容还是以大师为主。偶尔会有朋友开始通过办补习班来赚钱。从老师中能感觉到有纠结产生，因为有老师能买得起很贵的汽车。整体上情绪还是比较压抑与克制。2000年后，我突然才感觉自己比较穷，于是在朋友的指导下做了一年的服装生意，生意也没有亏钱，好玩却很累，又不是我想要的生活，还有我能感觉到自己这辈子能做成什么样，让人很沮丧。现在来看，2000年之前的感受还是学生式的激情，2000年之后是生活本身的激情。

／尹丽川 我的经历与你很相似。小时候也是被教导理想主义，被教导要服从顺从，要热爱一些空洞虚假的事物。但少年时代起，一切已经变化，各种经商浪潮、犬儒主义，谁也不再相信学校说的、报纸说的，乃至父母说的话。最终接触到外来文化，又接触到中国传统文化。人人生而敏感。从小我就对光天化日下、义正言辞的说辞，有深刻的怀疑。对社会怀疑，对人生怀疑，但又在禁锢之下长大。直到上了大学，听了摇滚乐，看了加缪和马尔克斯，那时才想到，这世上有着能互相理解的人，积攒多年的怀疑，转化成表达欲和一种质问、反抗的心情。

屠宏涛／ 我算是普通青年吧。我也对生活充满好奇和热爱。我觉得人只要能安静下来就会有成就。生活并不是谁可以预设的东西，所以在长大的过程中人就会总结经验。谁能有效地总结经验，同时吸收更新的经验就完美了。诗人的创作更依赖于个人敏锐的生活体验感吧。

／尹丽川 创作肯定来源于生存体验。不过，创作比生存体验更自由。在创作中，我不仅是我，还可以当任何其他人。我觉得根本上，是因为人性有共通处。

屠宏涛／ 我也觉得，我的创作对象就是我自己的生活。你的诗中有很多叛逆的意味。

／尹丽川 是的，也许这就是我所秉持的“质疑精神”。因为从小受的欺骗太多，被伤害了。

屠宏涛／ 你怎么会有那么强烈的感受，我现在觉得自己仍不够成熟。我好像不是太……不太清楚，我倒觉得艺术一直是个体的，说实话，我还没有看到比较明确的方式或是新的结构可以覆盖老一代的经验。70 年代出生的艺术家里还没有新的知识结构的参与来修正或覆盖老先生的方法。我倒不自卑，这需要些时间深入，从集体修养上“70后”要比之前的好很多，只要不是简单的概念移植、符号移植，新的艺术自然会生成。我觉得我们这代人的生存体验是很难用理性主义的概念来表达的。

我想这种理性主义，就是回到常识，回到生命常态吧。需要反抗的东西太多了，但艺术又不能沦为反抗的工具。对我个人来说，从创作初始就被贴上各种标签，“不确定性”也是一种标签。如果我还在创作，根本原因仅仅是我还有话想说。不管这话是针对社会，针对政治，还是个人体验。 /尹丽川

屠宏涛/ 这很好，不确定说明社会还有很多问题，人们不满足，很兴奋。如果事情都完全确定了，就没有发展的必要。中国的生活形态并不稳定，那我们都生活在一个未知的结构中。艺术对我来说算是用冒险和敏感来完成对当代的结构表述。因为冒险性，所以今天看来很可能是语意模糊，很难接受。其实这是很肯定的东西。这种结果肯定不是今天人自己判定的。只有未来的人经历完整的事件后，他才能清楚地看到哪个艺术家最清晰地表达出了他们时代的精神和社会结构。我想我会更加勇敢地进行对未知经验的探索。

我想我的文字和电影作品，最终是关注人与人的关系，人与世界的关系。了解别人才能了解自己。一个人是通过他人，和这个世界发生关系的。我的电影情怀归根结底是：让我们相依为命吧。我对当代艺术有些厌倦，就是因为被阐释得太多了。我不介意任何形态，仅仅分为喜欢的作品和不喜欢的作品。我曾写过，苦海无边，回头无岸，电影是我们的船。艺术就是这样。做艺术是以提炼的方式来修行。当然，对我来说，它也是世上最可爱的职业。艺术最终，起码我心中的艺术，是帮助我们明了人生，追寻觉悟。 /尹丽川

Rationalism Means Returning to Life's Normal State

A Dialogue between Tu Hongtao and Yin Lichuan

Tu Hongtao / As for the Cultural Revolution, it probably does not have much of a direct relation to me. From the time I was little I led a very ordinary life, and I was blessed with happiness.

In 1991 I went to Chongqing and began to live independently, getting a feel for many things you can't learn about in books. I remember that I used to like getting in fights and drinking beer. The school didn't have a television, but it had video games. We used rice coupons and grain coupons to get meals. If you liked a girl classmate, you would charm her by learning new popular songs from Hong Kong. At around that time, reading poetry started to become outmoded. In 1995 when I went to study in Hangzhou, we still did not see a big gap between rich and poor in our school. Our main topic of conversation was still the great masters. Once in a while, a classmate would make money by starting up a crammer school. Then something happened among the faculty members that gave you pause, because some of the teachers could buy very expensive cars. Overall, the mood was fairly repressed and self-restrained. In the year 2000 I suddenly felt that I was living in poverty. With guidance from friends I went into the garment business for a year. My business did not lose money: it was fun but exhausting, and it wasn't the life I wanted. What was more, I could see where it was leading and I realized that there were limits to how far I could go, which was a depressing thought. Now that I look back, what I felt before 2000 was the passion of a student. What I felt after that was the passion of life itself.

Yin Lichuan / My experience was quite similar to yours. When little I was also taught to be idealistic; I was taught to obey and defer to authority. I was told to feel ardent love for hollow, puffed-up things. But from my teen-age years on, great changes were underway. There was a wave of going into business, a wave of cynicism. Nobody believed any more what was said at school, what the newspapers said, what our parents said. Finally I came in contact with culture from abroad, and along with that I came in contact with traditional Chinese culture. People are born with natural sensitivity. I had always been deeply skeptical of didactic moral pronouncements. I doubted society and I doubted what we were living for, but I grew up in a confined setting. When I went to university I heard rock music; I read Camus and Marquez. Only then did it occur to me that in this world there can be people who really understand each other. All that pent-up doubt transformed into an expressive urge ... into a mood of questioning and opposition.

Tu Hongtao / I guess you could say I was an ordinary young man. I was full of curiosity and enthusiasm about life. I felt that if a person could just settle into doing something, he could achieve things. You cannot draw up a program for life, so the process of growing up has to be summed up by each person. The person who does the most effective summing up, who absorbs new experience to go along with it, deserves the admiration he gets. A poet's creative work relies on his keen feel for life experience.

Yin Lichuan / Creative work definitely has its source in life experience. However, creative work has freedom that life experience doesn't. In creative work I am not just myself, I can be someone else, because there is commonality in human nature.

Tu Hongtao / I also feel that the subject of my creative work is my own life. In your poems I see a strong mood of rebellion.

Yin Lichuan / Yes. Perhaps that comes from the "spirit of questioning" that I adhere to. I was deceived too much from an early age, and I feel the wounds.

Tu Hongtao / How can you have such intense feelings over that? Right now I feel that I'm still not mature enough. I don't have a clear idea yet. I feel that art has always been an individual thing. To tell the truth, I have not seen any distinct mode or new structure which can outdo the experience of our elders. Artists of the Seventies generation have not yet brought forth a new structure of knowledge that can revise or encompass the methods of our elders. This does not make me feel inferior; it takes time to deepen one's practice. In terms of cultivation, the Seventies generation overall is much better than the previous generations. As long as we don't go in for simple transplanting of concepts, or transplanting symbols, new art will naturally come into being. I feel that life experience of our generation cannot easily be conveyed using rationalistic ideas.

/ Yin Lichuan: I feel that rationalism is just getting back to common sense: it is returning to life's enduring state. There are too many things that need to be resisted, but art cannot sink to being a tool of resistance. As for me as an individual, since I began my creative work, I've had labels put on me. "Indefiniteness" is also a label. If I am still working creatively, the fundamental reason is that I still have something to say, regardless of whether it is aimed at society, politics, or experience.

Tu Hongtao / That's a good point. Indefiniteness shows there are still a lot of problems in society: people are not satisfied, so there is something to get excited about. If things were already definite, there would be no necessity for development. Our mode of life in China has still not stabilized, and so we live in a structure that has many unknowns. To me, art draws upon risk and sensitivity to give a structural account of our current era. Because it takes risks it may be seen as semantically vague and hard to accept from today's point of view. Actually, it may be an affirmative statement of something. But the value of such a statement is not for people of today to determine. Only people of the future, after having gone through the whole course of events, can see which artist conveyed the spirit of his time and the structure of his society most distinctly. I intend to carry on my explorations of unknown experiences more boldly than ever.

/ Yin Lichuan: I feel that my writings and film projects are ultimately concerned with relationships among people, or the relation of a person to the world. I have to understand others in order to understand myself. A person connects with the world by means of other people. The fundamental sensibility of my films is to call upon people to take care of each other. I am somewhat fed up with contemporary art, simply because there is too much interpretation. I don't care what the genre is: I only divide artworks into ones I like and ones I don't like. I once wrote: the bitter sea is boundless, turning about I see no shore. Films are my ship. So it is with art. In art you cultivate yourself as you distill expressive forms. Of course, I feel this is the most loveable profession in the world. Ultimately art helps us understand life and pursue enlightenment: at least this is true of art as it exists within my heart.

明月光　2009年　布面油画　180cm × 230cm

Moonlight　2009　oil on canvas　180cm×230cm

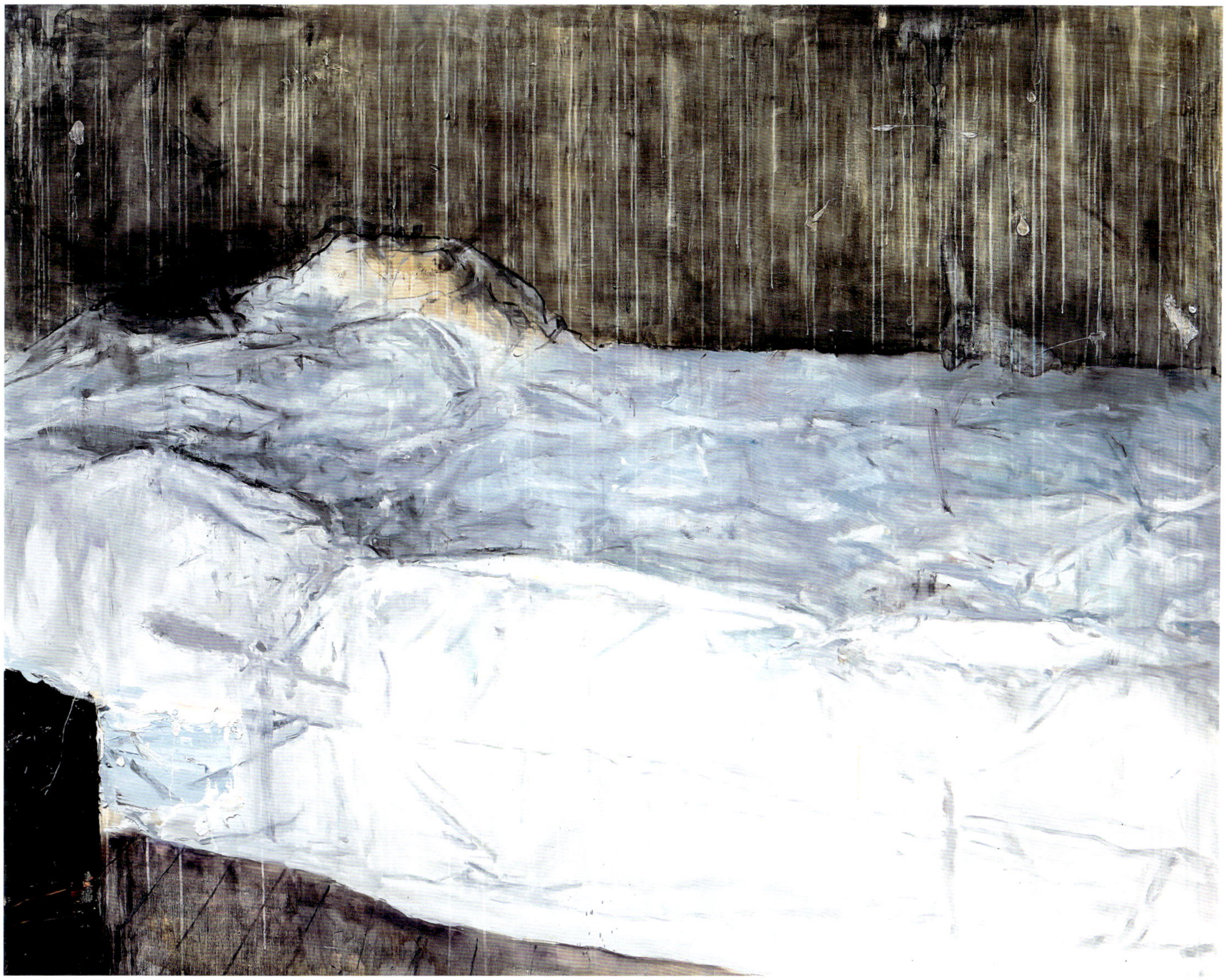

绿色风景　2010年　布面油画　155cm × 180cm

Green Landscape　2010　oil on canvas　155cm×180cm

乱卷　2010年　布面油画　150cm × 210cm

Chaotic Books　2010　oil on canvas　150cm×210cm

灰色风景　2010年　布面油画　155cm × 180cm

Grey Landscape　2010　oil on canvas　155cm × 180cm

康海涛
Kang Haitao

1976年生于重庆，2000年毕业于四川美术学院油画系。康海涛的"夜色"，将普通人习以为常的经验转化为陌生的视觉范式，在不确定感的视觉体验中营造了一种冷静、厚重而幽远的精神影像。从某种角度上说，康海涛是将绘画性发挥到极致，并进而使语言自身具有观念诉求的画家。这种特质，在流行化的图像浪潮中，显得尤为难得。

Born 1976 in Chongqing, graduated 2000 from Oil Painting Dept., Sichuan Fine Arts Institute. Kang's night-time views transform commonplace experience to an unfamiliar visual pattern. Amid a visual feel of indefiniteness, he shapes images that evoke a composed, deeply grounded, outward-opening spirit. Kang carries painterliness to its zenith, so that visual language itself poses conceptual challenges. These characteristics are all the more precious given the current tide of popularized imagery.

媒体人，举凡城市潮流、文化传播均有涉猎。“逃离北上广”话题发起人，789艺文节联合创立人。中国第一代Blogger，专注媒体与社会影响、网络传播的观察、研究与实践。

Innovator in a broad range of cultural media, initiator of web discussion forums, co-founder of 798 Art and Culture Festival, first generation Chinese blogger. He is a researcher and practitioner of new Internet communications, with a special interest in social influence of media.

寻找更加适合自己的生存方式

康海涛 | 李 劳

康海涛／ 我很少认真反思自己生存记忆的问题，对我来说，记忆中好像很多事情都是模模糊糊地就过来了。从小到大没有谁给你过特别大的生活压力，也没有谁给你明确的精神指引，要你必须去做什么，自己有很大的空间可以去选择自己的生活，而且这种选择变得更加宽阔和包容。它可以是很个人化的，也可以是涉及社会和政治的，但是这种状态中，好像又没有60年代出生的那一代人，是为了共同的理想在努力，他们可能更多关注的是各自心中的梦。

“70后”这一代人，思想成熟得更晚些，因为他们开始意识到个体存在的价值，开始真正关注自己的内心。不同的人，开始寻找更加适合自己的生存方式，重新开始探索新的生活。但是，怎样才能建立起新的价值观？它又怎样才能在这个时代找到自己的位置？这就注定了这种“回归”是漫长而艰苦的。我们这代人虽然有很强的自我认同感，但大都还有很强的社会责任感，这也是体现在他们身上严肃、理性的一面，怎样去平衡个体自由和社会责任之间的关系，也许是这一代人面临的一个很重要的问题。李劳你在文化传媒领域一定感触到更多的东西，你有着怎样的时代记忆呢？

李 劳／ 我真的不太清楚年代概念能不能真的发挥概括作用，但我很确信家庭、出身、成长经历对一个人或他的创作的影响会很大。对我自己来说，生于一个北方农村，小时候有电线但只有下半夜有电（因为电力要优先供给城市和工业），所以我大部分时间用来读很烂的杂志（比如《故事会》）和听收音机。如果没有书和收音机，我不会离开出生地成长为一个想太多事的人，我想我会有更多质朴的快乐和痛苦。

另外，我的父母很质朴，他们话很少，只知道勤奋劳动，然后在过年的时候鼓励我好好读书，我小时候读书好是因为想让很辛苦的他们高兴一点。当然，这个经历让后来来到城市生活的人带来很多东西，有很多正面的，也有另外的一些，比如你会看到同一个中国，有人辛苦一辈子到70岁还不能退休，有人可以一夜花掉别人几年的收入，而这种差距背后的理由是不能拿到台面上来说的。这种观察给我一种巨大的痛苦感。这种经历令我发现，屁股决定脑袋，我非常能理解杨继绳、于建嵘这些学者为什么能做那些事。这种反差的背后反而是一种淡漠，无论是享有利益的还是被剥夺利益的都很淡漠，但我做不到，体会到一种巨大的文化和情感上的悲怆。

康海涛／ 这似乎是一种很无可奈何的状态。所以我希望自己每天都能尽量真实地去生活，若干年后回头看看划出的这道轨迹，也就是自己的所在。

李 劳／ 我分析过自己、家庭、成长经历甚至小学时的同学关系，当然还有DNA决定了自己，决定了自己是什么人，做什么样的事，没有一个样板，但一定不会超出一个范围。你觉得自己的创作与生存体验之间是一种怎样的关系？

康海涛／ 创作来源于自己内心的真实感受。一开始画“晚上”就是觉得夜晚里的事物非常美，很宁静、很神秘，静静地散发着某种强大的生命力，并没有想赋予它太多的意义。如果要去分析它，可能和自己热爱自然，喜欢简单有关，甚至和逃避现实都有很大的关系，因为现实确实有太多的喧嚣和过于物质化的东西。就“夜晚”的创作来说，我确实想在以宁静、神秘为基调的绘画中去探索一些可能性，并希望这样的绘画能触动到和我有共同体验的一些人。不知道你怎么看？

你是一个非常散淡的人，应该与你的家庭和成长经历有关。而对我来说，动荡、反差、针锋相对、势不两立这些状态是我经常体会到的，既痛苦又迷恋。无论在人生看法还是审美上都是这样。我写文章、做报道、发微博，带领一小队媒体人去做一件事，凡此种种都不是没来由的，目的很明确。你觉得“70后”艺术家有着怎样的特征？ ／李　劳

康海涛／ “自我”、“多元”、“理性”这几个词或许可以用来概括这个群体的艺术表现。因为这一代人没有经历过文革，所以意识形态的影响在他们身上的烙印并没有那么深，再加上80年代西方各种艺术思潮的纷纷涌入，给艺术的生长带来了活力，所以“70后”一代的艺术家整体呈现出“自我”而“多元”的格局。意识形态不重，但并不代表没有影响，从父母身上，从周围的环境或多或少都能感觉得到它的存在，上一代人的理想主义精神在他们身上也有所延续，所以他们对生活总是带有一份责任感，好多作品中总能留下理性思考的痕迹。

作为一个“70后”，我觉得我们是放不开的一群人，既抱着理想主义的尾巴，又被消费主义侵染，很多时候游移不定。当然我们最大的优势是体会了1979年之后的整个变革，这种变革给我们带来的影响会超过其他代际的人。我相信，再过些年肯定会有伟大的作品诞生，记述30多年来发生的事，给中国人带来的撕裂与挤压。杭春晓提出“不确定”的概念，你是怎么看的？ ／李　劳

康海涛／

我觉得“不确定性”是一种实验探索的精神，是事物生生不息的状态。从历史的角度来看，意识形态的东西开始慢慢消解，再加上全球化的进程越来越快，东西方文化的交流变得越来越频繁，各种艺术观念和思潮相互碰撞，给艺术创作带来了更多的可能性，我们这一代人的创造空间更大、更自由了。就创作本身来说，创作者的每一次行为都必须最大程度地去清空自己的头脑，让自己和未知连接在一起，“探索未知”其实就是一种“不确定性”，在这种状态里面才会有真正的创造力产生。一件好的作品对作者和观者来说都会有这种不确定感，在不同的时间和空间里面去阅读它会有不同的体验和感受，每一次的阅读都会是前一次的延伸和扩展，都能得到新的收获。就像一个转动的球体一样，我们随时都能看到它不同的方位，但这个球体本身又是极其圆融和耐人寻味的。

就关于“夜晚”的绘画来说吧，一开始并没有想过要去确切表达什么东西，晚上的感受对于我来说只是一个出发点，或者说是一种可能性，我期待着让作品自己去呈现一种状态，并且这种状态一直在变化着。

“夜晚”的绘画也是自己“心力”的锻炼过程，一点一点地去接近某种深度的宁静。这一点一点的变化，是绘画过程的内在变化，也是绘画继续下去的精神支撑，至于作品中呈现出来的其他内容，就像长在骨头上的肉一样，它会让作品更加立体、丰富和完整。

我觉得当代艺术的发展应该更加自由和多元，不应该拘泥于任何一种形式，内容上甚至可以是跨学科的，只要能够表达得足够彻底。艺术最终要解决的就是“自由表达”的问题，如何才能最大程度地去表达自己，这是最难也是最值得去做的事情。每个人的意识状态不一样，对生活的感受也不一样，只有当你的表达完全成为你自己的时候，艺术才能散发出最强大的力量，这种力量才会渗透到生命中最微小的角落。

／李　劳

谈到自由与多元的时候，我内心其实有些恐惧，就像一觉醒来漂在四面都望不到边的大海上，可能我是一个需要界定来确定自己存在的人。你谈到“夜晚”——说你期待作品自己去呈现，有没有这种恐惧就是你的作品在做你，而不是你在做作品。我说“作品在做你”这个句子的时候，背景是对现代生活的思考，我觉得大部分人在大部分时间是在“被生活”着，而不是他们自以为地在主导自己的生活，他想买什么，爱好什么，甚至找一个什么样的人相爱结婚，其实都是受政治、商业、传媒各种机构释放的信号的影响而形成的。我对这个常常会警醒，像Neo在矩阵里头发现自己是一段写好的程序一样。老实说，对这个我十分焦虑。

文革结束之际，权威的消解就开始了，到后来对所有权威甚至智力的东西也开始消解和逆反——因为它们在特定的时间内扮演了很不光彩的角色。这种消解到现在仍在继续，但到了“90后”不用消解了，因为那些东西基本上没给他们造成太深的影响，他们又不看《新闻联播》。

Finding A Mode of Existence More Suited to the Self

A Dialogue between Kang Haitao and Li Lao

Kang Haitao / I seldom reflect seriously on my memories of life. My memories of passing things are hazy for the most part. From an early age, nobody put a great deal of pressure on me, and nobody gave me clear spiritual guidance or told me what I must do. I had a fair amount of space to choose a life for myself, and that space grew even broader and more tolerant over time. It could be a very individual space, or it could touch upon society and politics. We were not like members of the Sixties generation, who made concerted efforts for the sake of ideals. We are probably more concerned with the dream that each of us carries in his or her heart.

Maturity for the Seventies generation came somewhat belatedly, because we started becoming aware of the value of individual existence; we started being truly concerned with our own inner lives. Each different person began searching for a mode of existence suited to him or herself. We began once again to explore new ways of life. But how was a new value system to be established? How could a place be found for such a thing in this era? Thus our homecoming was fated to be prolonged and difficult. Though people of our generation have a strong sense of personal identity, most of us also have a strong sense of social responsibility, which can be seen in our earnestness and rational tendencies. How to find a balance between individual freedom and social responsibility is perhaps one of the major issues facing people of this generation. Li Lao, your work in cultural media must put you in contact with many interesting things. What are your memories of our era?

Li Lao / I am not clear as to whether the concept of generation can really encapsulate all that much. But I strongly believe that family, class background, and growth experiences have a big influence on a person and his creative work. In my case, I was born in a northern village. When I was little we had an electric line, but we only had electricity during the second half of the night (because cities and industries received preferential allotment of electric power). Most of my time was spent reading pulp fiction magazines and listening to the radio. If not been for books and radio, I never would have tilled a new piece of ground and grown up to become someone who thinks too much. I would have experienced more unpretentious joys and pain.

My father and mother were unpretentious people. They did not talk a lot; they only knew how to labor diligently. While resting at New Year they would urge me to do well in my studies. I studied hard, to give my hard-working parents a bit of happiness. Having gone through such experiences, a person who relocates to the city will bring certain things with him, some of them positive, some not so positive. For instance I see that we all live in this nation of China, where some people work past age 70 and can't retire, while other people can spend the yearly incomes of several people in a single evening. Yet the reasons for such a discrepancy cannot be put on the table for discussion. Observing such things causes me to feel tremendous pain. My experiences helped me to realize that "where your butt sits determines what your brain thinks." I can definitely understand why scholars like Yang Jisheng and Yu Jianrong did what they did [1]. Behind this great discrepancy is indifference. Whether those who derive benefit or those who are deprived of benefit—all of them show indifference about this matter. But I cannot do it. I feel tremendous grief, both culturally and emotionally.

Kang Haitao / This is something we have to resign ourselves to, so I hope to live every day in an authentic way. After a number of years, after I turn and look at the track I have made, I will be looking back at where I am now.

Li Lao / I analyze myself and find that I am determined by family, growth experiences, even relations with classmates in primary school, and of course there is my DNA. These determine the person I am and what I do. There is no fixed pattern, but these things will stay within a certain scope. What relation do you feel there is between your life experience and creative work?

Kang Haitao / Creative work originates in one's genuine inner feelings. When I started painting "Evenings," I felt that things at night-time had a lovely appearance, so tranquil and mysterious, and that they emanated a powerful living presence. I did not want to confer too much meaning on them. If you analyze this, it could have been related to my love of nature or my fondness for simplicity; it even had a lot to do with my escapist streak, because reality is definitely too full of noise and materialism. As for my creation of "Evenings," I really wanted to explore the possibilities in paintings that were keyed to stillness and mystery. I was hoping that such paintings would touch people who had kindred feelings. I wonder how you view this.

You are an easy-going person, which is probably related to your family and growth experiences. My normal state of awareness is one of upheaval, discrepancy, clashing forces, and antagonism. It is painful, but it also exerts fascination on me. My view of human life and my aesthetic sense are both like this. I write articles, do reporting, post things on my mini-blog. I have a media crew under my guidance, and our projects all have clear sources and clear aims. / Li Lao

What characteristics do you feel are shared by Seventies generation artists?

Kang Haitao / "Self-directed," 'pluralist,' "rational"—I think these keywords can all encapsulate the artistic expression of this group. Because they did not go through the Cultural Revolution, ideology did not leave such a deep mark on them. In addition we saw wave after wave of art trends come flooding in, which imparted vitality to art in its growing phase. So artists of the Seventies generation present a "self-directed" and "pluralistic" configuration. Ideology's weight is not crushing, but that does not mean it is without influence. One can feel its existence, to some extent, in one's parents' attitudes and in surrounding circumstances. The idealistic spirit of the previous generation has found continuance in this generation's character. This is why they invariably have a sense of responsibility about life, and traces of rational thinking are seen in many of their works.

As a member of the Seventies generation, I feel that we are a group that finds it hard to detach ourselves. Not only do we keep holding on to the tail end of idealistic thinking, we feel the encroachments of consumerism, and we often vacillate between the two. Of course our biggest advantage is that we experienced the whole process of reform since 1979. The extent of influence that was absorbed since the reforms cannot be equaled by any other generation. I believe that in a few years great works will come into being, to give an account of the wrenching, teeming events that happened during the past thirty years. / Li Lao

What do you think about the concept of "indefiniteness" that was proposed by Hang Chunxiao?

Kang Haitao / I feel that "indefiniteness" is a spirit of experimentation and exploration. It is a state of ongoing life that makes things new. From a historical angle, ideological constraints have been dissolving, the advance of globalization has been speeding up, and East-West cultural exchanges are increasing in frequency. All sorts of art ideas and currents have been colliding, bringing more possibilities for artistic, creative work. Our generation's space for creative work has gotten bigger and freer. As for creative work itself, each act by a creative person requires that the mind be emptied [of preconceived notions], to link oneself up with the unknown. Exploring the unknown is a matter of indefiniteness. Only in this state does genuine creativity arise. A good artwork has this sense of the indefinite, both for the auteur and the viewer. When perused in different times and settings, it will give different experiences and feelings. Each perusal can be an extension or broadening of the previous one, always yielding something new. It is like a rotating sphere: over time we see different locations on its surface, but it is an integral entity with its own intriguing wholeness. As for paintings like the "Night-Time" series, I did not think at first of expressing any particular message. My perceptions of evening were only a point of departure, perhaps a possibility. I anticipated letting the works themselves present a special state, and this state kept undergoing change.

Painting the "Night-Time" series was a process of tempering my "force of mind," as I approached that deep stillness bit by bit. That incremental change happened internally during the painting process, and gave me spiritual support that let me continue painting. As for other content that appeared in the works, that was like flesh growing on bones to make the works more layered, rich and complete. I think the development of contemporary art should move toward freedom and plurality. It should not be bogged down in any certain form, and it can even be multi-disciplinary in content, as long as it expresses something thoroughly. What art ultimately has to solve is the problem of free expression—that is, how to express oneself as freely as possible. This is the hardest thing, and the worthiest to pursue. Each person's state of consciousness is different, his perceptions of life are different. Only when you and your expression are merged can art give off a powerful force, a force that will reach into the subtlest corners of life.

/ Li Lao

When we talk about freedom and plurality, I have a fear deep inside, as if one might wake up adrift with a boundless ocean on all sides. Perhaps I need to define certain bounds for myself. You speak of your "Night-Time" and say that you anticipate the self-manifestation of the artwork. Do you ever have a fear that the artwork is painting you, instead of you creating the artwork? When use the words "the artwork is painting you," the background of what I say is my thinking about modern life. I feel that for most people most of the time, we are "being lived" rather than taking charge of our own lives. What a person thinks, what his hobbies are, or even the kind of person he seeks to marry—it all takes shape under influence of signals that are emitted by government and business and media. I try to remain wary of this, like Neo when he discovered he was a segment of code in the matrix. In truth I have considerable anxiety over this.

After Mao Zedong, the era of deification in politics began to dissolve. Later the grip of authority and even intellectual dominance began to dissolve and produce a backlash, because at a certain period, those things had played a dishonorable role. This dissolution is still going on. But when it comes to the Nineties generation, there is no need for such dissolution, because those things did not have an overly large influence on that generation. They don't even watch the network news.

[1] Yang Jisheng's book Mubei (Tombstone) documents the famines of the early 1960s during which over 30,000,000 people starved. (Tiandi Tushu Youxian Gongsi, Hong Kong, 2008) . Yu Jianrong, professor in the Rural Development Research Institute at the Academy of Social Sciences, is a vocal advocate of farmers' and workers' interests through his blog on the Internet. His books include Chinese Working Class Conditions: A Field Study in Anyuan.

老厂房　2008年　纸板丙烯　102cm × 201cm

Old Factory　2008　acrylic on paperboard　102cm×201cm

空地　2011年　纸板丙烯　90cm × 160cm

Glade　2011　acrylic on paperboard　90cm×160cm

树　2011年　纸板丙烯　126cm × 93cm

Tree　2011　acrylic on paperboard　126cm×93cm

街口　2011年　纸板丙烯　134cm × 101cm

Street　2011　acrylic on paperboard　134cm×101cm

管 勇
Guan Yong

1975年出生于山东菏泽，2003年毕业于天津美术学院油画系，获硕士学位。毕业前后创作的“幽默与经典”系列作品，于2004年“中国新锐绘画展”中广为关注。其后，他的创作一直以某种色彩象征感著称，且多呈现为开放性的视觉结构，通常以对知识分子的反思为出发点，具有一种对文化形成历史的追问意识。近年来创作转向对于视觉呈现原则的反思与审视，多借助镜像制造带有悖论的视觉线索，从而通过这种视觉线索的重构，显现了极为冷静地观看世界的态度，并于“逻辑化”与“非逻辑化”的悖论中，向观者提示了一种关于“真实”、“虚幻”的哲学化理性审视，是“70后”强调理性审视的代表性艺术家之一。

Born 1975 in Heze, Shandong, graduated 2003 from Oil Painting Dept., Tianjin Fine Arts Institute. After graduation he created the series "Humor and Classics" and attracted wide notice in the "Pathbreakers of Chinese Painting Exhibition." Later his works were known for symbolic value of color, presenting open-ended visual structures which took the reflective thought of intellectuals as a starting point. His work shows a sense of inquiry into how culture takes shape as history. In recent years, he has has shifted toward visual renditions of his reflections about principles. He draws on mirror images to present visual paradoxes. Through his restructuring of visual linearity, he conveys a rigorous attitude toward the world of seeing. In his paradoxes of logicality and illogicality, he involves viewers in philosophical stock-taking with regards to "truthfulness" and "illusion."

管 勇

Guan Yong

皮 三

Pi San

1971年生于山西，双子座。1996年毕业于山西大学美术系油画专业。2005年创办互象动画公司。现居北京。代表作品有《泡芙小姐》、《哐哐日记》，贾樟柯电影《世界》中的动画片段，左小祖咒、万晓利、苏阳等音乐人的动画MV……所参与艺术展览有：2010年“从电影看现代艺术展”（深圳）、2009年“FAT ART目耳计划当代艺术展”（北京）、2006年“江湖中国现代艺术展”（美国纽约）、1999年“新锐的目光——1970年前后出生的一代”（北京、广州等）等。

Born 1971 in Shanxi in the sign of Gemini, graduated 1996 from Fine Arts Dept., Shanxi University with a major in oil painting. In 2006 Pi San founded Huxiang Anime Company. He now lives in Beijing. His representative works include *Miss Puff* and *Quanger*, plus anime sequences in Jia Zhangke's film *The World*. He has made music videos for musicians including Zuoxiao Zuzhou, Wan Xiaoli and Su Yang. Exhibitions in include "View From Film Modern Art Exhibition" 2010, Shenzhen; "FAT ART Eye Ear Project Contemporary Art Expo" 2009, Beijing; "Rivers and Lakes Modern Chinese Art Exhibition" 2006, New York; "Pathbreaking Vision--The 1970s Generation" 1999, Guangzhou and Beijing.

所谓的真实没有意思

管 勇 | 皮 三

皮 三／ 你对文革有什么记忆？

我只有一些模糊的印象，大约记得领袖去世的时候，到处都是标语。现在一些比较偏远的地区，还有那种东西。 ／管 勇

皮 三／ 我仔细回想过文革，因为我家在文革的时候受过冲击。文革对于上代人而言，是一个特别疼的疤。对我来说，文革特别像荒诞剧，在我们身上多多少少都留下了一些痕迹。文革就像是一件特别的作品，我们这代人表现文革也显得很奇怪。在我的童年记忆里，有很多局部的点，现在被放大之后，就显得特别荒诞。

我们的文革记忆，可能跟年龄更小的人相比，感觉不一样。他们很可能理解为一个符号，诸如绿军装。而我们的上一代人，他们有切身的体验，文革就是他们生命中的一个组成部分。我觉得文革并不好面对，因为你不知道它到底是什么样的情况。有些人讲文革也很好，因为对于过往的记忆都伴随着美化的；也有人从来不愿意讲，可能因为对他伤害比较大。他不愿意回忆，不愿意面对这段历史，可能还是因为不到时间。我们理解起来就会比较困难，那个东西还是挺抽象的，你知道它确实发生过，而且非常荒谬。但是到底是什么东西导致这些个荒谬，或者说在那种环境下的人，又是一种什么样的状态，这些东西都太抽象，说不清楚。而且，我们整个的环境也回避这个东西。我说的回避，涉及社会、人性、权力运动或者涉及文化形态，甚至和我们的传统文化都有一定的关系。 ／管 勇

皮 三／ 是的。我觉得这里存在一个如何面对历史的态度的问题。有一次一个朋友就问我：喜欢听什么名家的古典音乐？我想了想，不知道该怎么回答。我小学时候听《小螺号》，大部分是革命歌曲，后来也听过崔健的摇滚乐，还是那种打口带。所谓的美育，可以说基本上是空白。后来逐渐接触到一些东西，很杂，可能四大名著与《百年孤独》是一起看的。可以回忆的内容，真的是非常少。

确实是这样的。我们所接受的信息，整体缺乏系统性。像打口带这种东西，本来就是片段式地在我们之间传播着，有可能产生了什么影响，但是很难说得清楚。上大学的时候，我们也能看到学校组织放映的一些文艺片，现在想也是很优秀的电影，像《天生杀人狂》，都是挺棒的片子。我感觉有很多，蛮激进的。 ／管 勇

皮 三／ 我记得电影《少林寺》，不知道看过多少遍，因为没其他东西看。不过，我们眼界还是开阔了一点，还是接触到了很多西方的东西。

我们那时候听的音乐，感觉比现在的质量要高。当时听的“大门”、“恐怖海峡”，都是特牛的乐队。 ／管 勇

皮　三／ 现在还是有好的东西，但是我们不怎么听。如果说荒诞，就像同时看的金庸，又同时听的乐队，都是一起发生在我们身上，非常自然。现在一些人的兴趣很集中，爱好收集的特别专业。我们那时候就显得特别不专业。各有好处吧。因为我们当时也没得选择，现在更多元和自由。我一直认为，“不确定性”对我特别重要。我是特别讨厌复制和正确性的人。前些天有一个东方论坛的活动，我们的评委是汪建伟老师，他说的几句话我印象很深。关于确定性、正确性的问题，这个跟年龄没关系，老汪岁数很大，但是一直保持不确定和反抗正确的态度。我们对于审美或者对于文化态度，我们只是做不确定状，还是我们有不确定的勇气，这是两个概念。我们只是表面上呈现某一个状态，但是将我的工作方式认为是不确定的，这是另外一个问题。你在个人作品的创作上，承不承认有一个什么态度？

管　勇／ 简单讲，保持开放的状态，这东西确实很难。至于怎么做，包括落实到什么样的方法论，肯定也是这样。“不确定”这个词也是很挺死板的东西，但这个东西不只是说一说那么简单，其实它背后涉及整个的知识系统。就像20世纪的哲学，特别20世纪后期的哲学，整个与现代主义、古典主义哲学，完全是扭转方向。不确定确实是比较重要的面向，里面包含着一个知识系统，不是简单说说就可以的，不是做个姿态就可以的。至于说这个姿态到底是什么样的，有时候也不太重要。作品的质量，有时候取决于一个系统性的东西，它需要系统化，需要深入化，而不是一种感觉，更加不可能只是一个姿态的东西。我认为个人的理想主义也是很重要的，但是总难以做到。就像刚才我们聊的，它是非常复杂和混乱的。我经常感觉自己非常弱，因为缺乏知识的体系。这种状况无论是做作品的时候，还是看其他人的东西的时候，我有时候能感觉到一种吃力感。

皮　三／ 我年轻时候特别爱看哲学，但是现在杂志为主。我是行动主义者，事情要落实到行动才有效。前不久尤伦斯黄建伟的“黄灯”展我挺喜欢，他的行动力我特别欣赏。我说的不确定，就是行动性，而不是一个概念放在我的书架里。我做的《哐哐》，觉得还是跟自己的性格有关系，我不想重复，就想否定自己，于是我做《泡芙小姐》。复制自己，未必能获得自己想要的东西，未必能卖多少钱，市场就是这样的。没有人是傻子，你变成标签人家就买你？不一定。“70后”就是没标签化，本来你就没有资格拥有一个标签，正在被忽略的时候是特别好的时候，也是自己可以乱搞、胡搞的时候。对了，你读书的时候有没有理想？

管　勇／ 应该说直到上大学的时候还有，现在是彻底没有了。理想都是骗人的。

皮　三／ 呵呵。我觉得我还是有理想的，要比我们的同事或者年轻一代有理想，我对企业、对我个人有理想，我对文化有理想。我去年做了一个动画论坛，采访的时候很多媒体问我为什么做这个活动。因为我们公司出钱，也没做宣传，动画公司不挣钱，穷得叮当响。我最后没法解释，我后来想我是个理想主义者，我对这个行业是有理想的所以才做这个事情。我自己确实这样想。

你谈的可能是责任心。我理解的理想，就要落实到具体，比如生活或者事业……这个也不靠谱，似乎总是想象的东西。我们经历得太多，到最后就变了，完全不是开始的那个东西。我认为，现在大家没有一个相对统一、相对大的价值观，就会导致也不需要抱团，所以我们的独立性越来越强，各干各的，所以可能不会出现群体性特别强的东西。 /管　勇

皮　三/ 我自小就知道，要顺从自己的兴趣做事。但到今天，我就发现所谓的“顺着”并不存在，应该是已经预设好的一些东西。在每个转折的时候，我都会刻意采取别人往左我往右。我搞不清这是环境的影响还是自己的性格决定的。我经常反思自己的作品，当有新的东西吸引我的时候，会激发我的创作点，但是我不确定创作点是不是属于我自己的。我是怀疑主义者，我就会怀疑自己，然后就停了。我一直鄙视自己，总是按兴趣玩。周围的朋友有做电影，做的特深沉的，贾樟柯那种特别人文，还有作家写的很深刻，摇滚的又是特别狠。我觉得自己怎么没正形，以前我瞧不起自己这个性格，后来我想我就不能瞎过，就把自己不靠谱、不着调、爱开玩笑的东西表现出来，然后做了《哐哐》。“70后”这代人分化特别明显，就是因为不确定性，各个方向的，因为没定性，也就没主义，他长大的那个阶段就是没主义的阶段，没办法。

你做作品的感觉是越来越紧张，而我的原则是放松，越来越放松。原来我还相信作品和现实之间有一种什么关系，现在彻底不信了。相信——这个东西不健康。我们看一个作品的时候，会想它是什么意思。其实，又有什么意义？我也不知道是什么，我认为那都是不必要的。假设我们画一个苹果，你问我是什么意思，我也不知道什么意思。因为这个意思不重要，它天生携带某种意思，它已经有意思了。艺术品往往是这样的，要放松，我是减弱或者彻底拿掉它跟某种现实的对应关系，我觉得非常不必要。我感觉优秀的作品，艺术家其实也是一个幻想，跟真实不真实好像没关系，他激发的永远是其他的东西：大概是观众在看这个东西时的感受。这时候不需要任何其他的东西。我研究生毕业后，教了几年大学，到后来不教了，烦了。因为一开始还理想主义，想教好课，到后来就发现这完全不可能。因为这个体制本身的设计，不可能教出好的东西：你即使认为是好的，他马上会抵消掉变成另外的。我认为我们都没有什么选择，你毫无选择。实际上选择是骗人的事，没有选择就有答案了。你感觉有选择的时候，我感觉有问题。我们都迷惑。 /管　勇

皮　三/ 对了，我看你最近的作品一直在画书，很有意思。我有一阶段挺爱画书，我周围人说我装什么知识分子。

一说书，就与知识分子联系在一起。我开始画的时候完全不是这样。我画的是自己的书架。我只是对书放在书架上，产生水平的线和垂直的线，感觉特别有意思。我要的画出来的就是这个。 /管　勇

皮　三/ 我的书架跟你很像。我觉得在深层里面，可能有很多习惯的认同。

So-Called Genuineness Holds No Interest

A Dialogue between Guan Yong and Pi San

Pi San / What are your memories of the Cultural Revolution?

Guan Yong / I only have hazy impressions. Mostly I remember when leaders passed away, mourning pronouncements would be put up everywhere. Now in some remote spots you can still find them.

Pi San / I've given some thought to the Cultural Revolution, because my family suffered a negative impact then. For the previous generation, the Cultural Revolution left a very painful scar. As for me, it was like a work of absurdist theater, and to some extent it left marks on me. The Cultural Revolution was like a special kind of artwork, and my generation's way of expressing it is quite odd. My childhood memories hold many partial views or isolated points, and when magnified they are especially absurd.

Guan Yong / Our Cultural Revolution memories probably have a different feel than memories of people a few years younger than us. They probably understand that period as a symbol, such as an olive drab outfit. But people of the previous generation went through it first hand; it was part of their lives. I feel the Cultural Revolution is not easy to confront, because you really do not know what conditions were then. Some people say good things about it, because there is a tendency to beautify memories of the past. Some people are unwilling to talk about it, perhaps because they suffered too much. A person may be unwilling to remember, unwilling to confront that segment of history, because the time may not be right. That makes it difficult to understand. It is hard to get at something so abstract: you know it actually happened, and you know that it was extremely absurd, but as for what might have led to such absurdity, or what state people got into under such circumstances—these things have been left on an abstract level and cannot be clearly stated. What is more, our environment avoids the subject. The avoidance I speak of has to do with our society, with human nature, with operations of power and cultural patterns; it is even related somehow to our traditional culture.

Pi San / That's right. I feel this is a problem of attitudes about confronting history. Once a friend asked me what classical music I like to listen to. I thought about it but didn't know how to answer him. I remember listening to "The Little Conch"…. Mostly I listened to revolutionary songs. Later I listened to Cui Jian, and to rock bands on pirated tapes. There was a big blank in terms of what you would call "aesthetic education." Later I came in contact with a grab bag of things. I probably read China's four famous traditional novels[1] at the same as One Hundred Years of Solitude. What I recall of the content is negligible.

Guan Yong / I know what you mean. There was nothing systematic about the information we absorbed. Like those pirated tapes—they were passed around among us in a haphazard way, and they probably had some kind of influence, but it's hard to say clearly what it was. While going to college we were able to watch screenings of art films organized on campus. Looking back, I think there were some outstanding films, like Natural Born Killers; those were great films, in my view, some pretty radical works of film.

Pi San / I remember the film Shaolin Temple. I saw it umpteen times, because there was nothing going on. But our horizons were expanded somewhat. We did come in contact with a lot of Western things, after all.

Guan Yong / I feel that the quality of music we listened to was better than music now. We used to listen to the "Doors" and "Dire Straits." Those were tremendous bands.

Pi San /

There are good things now, but we don't seek them out as much. If you want to talk about absurdity, what about reading Jin Yong's martial arts novels at the same time we listened to rock music? All those things converged upon us, yet it was all very natural. Now some people are highly focused on their interests: they become quite professional about their hobbies and collections. Back then we did not seem professional at all. I suppose there are advantages to both ways. Back then we had no choice but to do things that way. Now things are more pluralistic, and you're free to do more. I feel that "indefiniteness" is quite important. I don't care for people who get into standardization or correctness. A few days ago there was an event called the Oriental Forum, and my teacher Wang Jianwei was on the judging committee. He made a few remarks that left a deep impression on me. The problem of definiteness and correctness has nothing to do with age. Old Wang is old in years, but he keeps an indefinite attitude and resists correctness. With respect to aesthetic and cultural attitudes, either we just strike an indefinite pose, or we have the courage to be indefinite in a real way—these are two different ideas. You may present a semblance, but if you are going to approach your mode of work as something indefinite, this becomes a different issue. How about you? Do you admit to having a certain attitude in your creative work?

/ Guan Yong

To put it simply, it's not easy to maintain an open-ended state. As for what steps you take, how you settle on the right methodology, that is bound to be difficult too. The term "indefinite" is a fairly rigid notion. It's not something that can be summed up in a few simple words. Actually, behind there is a whole system of knowledge involved behind that idea. For instance if you look at Twentieth Century philosophy, especially in the late part of the century, it goes off in a direction that's counter to modernism and classical philosophy overall. Indefiniteness is certainly an important orientation, one which contains a system of knowledge that you cannot reduce to a few simple words. Simply adopting it as a stance is not enough. As for explaining what this stance might entail, maybe that is not all that important. The quality of an artwork is often decided by a system lying behind it. That requires a systematic approach; it requires in-depth inquiry. It is not just a feeling, any more than it could be a matter of just taking a stance.

I feel that an idealistic tendency is important, but it is so hard to carry out. As we were saying a little while ago, it is quite complex and hard to sort out. I often feel that I'm quite weak because I lack a system of knowledge. Due to this condition, whether working on my own pieces or viewing others' pieces, I sometimes feel that it's tough going.

Pi San /

When I was young I loved reading philosophy, but now my main reading is magazines. I am a believer in action. Only when something is carried out can it be effective. I really liked Huang Jianwei's "Yellow Lamp" show at Ullens Gallery recently. I really appreciate his power of action. I am not putting it clearly. It is tangible action, as opposed to an idea that you put on your bookshelf. I felt that my piece "Quanger" fit well with my personality. I did not wish to repeat it, so I wanted to negate myself, and that is why I did **Miss Puff. Even if you re-duplicate yourself, you may not get what you are after: you may not be able to sell your works for much—that is how the market is. People are not stupid: they are not going to buy you just because you label yourself. Not likely. The Seventies generation does not get labeled; you are not qualified to have a label put on you anyway. The time when you're being rejected is the best time for you: you can mess around any way you see fit. What about you? Did you have ideals about your studies?

/ Guan Yong

I'l have to say that until I went to university I still had ideals, but now they're thoroughly gone. Ideals are a deception.

Pi San /

Heh-heh. I feel that I have ideals after all. Compared to my colleagues and the younger generation, I have ideals. I have ideals about business, about myself as a person, and about culture. Last year I held a forum about anime. During the interviews, a lot of reporters asked me why I would put on such an event. You see, our company was paying for it, and it had not been advertized. Our anime company doesn't make money: it hardly has two coins to rub together. In the end I had no way to explain, and later it occurred to me that I'm an idealist. I have ideals about this occupation, or I would not do such things. I am convinced that is why.

/ Guan Yong

What you're talking about may be a sense of responsibility. As I understand ideals, they have to be implemented in concrete ways, whether in your life or in your vocation ... But they are too dicey. It seems to end up being a matter of imagination. We've been through it many times, seeing how they change in the end to something utterly unlike they were at the beginning. I feel that we all lack a relatively unified, overarching value system, which makes it unnecessary to stick with one group. So our independent-mindedness is getting stronger. Each person is doing his own thing, so we're not going to see a strong group dynamic.

Pi San /

From an early age I knew enough to follow my own interests. But now I'm starting to discover that there is no such thing as "following." It must be that some things are already set up ahead of time. At each pivotal moment, I always make a point of turning left when others turn right. I can't figure out whether this is influenced by my environment, or whether it is decided by my personality. I often reflect on my own works: when something new exerts an attraction on me, it rouses a creative focus in me, but I can't be sure whether that focal point belongs to me or not. Being an eternal skeptic, I feel skeptical about myself, so then I stop. I feel disdain toward myself because I only play with things for as long as they hold my interest. In my circle there are friends who make films with a great deal of gravitas, like Jia Zhangke whose films are strongly humanistic. I know writers who write with profundity, and rock musicians who play the edgiest music. I wonder why I have no proper shape. I used to look down on my own personality, but then I realized I cannot be something I'm not. So I started to express this dicey, chameleon-like, jokester side of myself. Then I created "Quanger." It is very apparent the way the Seventies generation has been differentiating into various paths, it must be due to indefiniteness. There are all sorts of orientations, having no set configuration, not knowing what they're supposed to do. The stage when you're growing up is the stage when you don't know what to do, but that's the way it is.

/ Guan Yong

When creating an artwork, your feeling seems to become increasingly tense. For me, the principle is to let go, to be more and more relaxed. Originally I still believed that the piece had some relation to reality. Now I don't believe it at all. To believe it would be unhealthy. When we look at an artwork, we think about what it means. Actually, it does not have to have a meaning, does it? I don't know what it's supposed to mean, and I don't feel that it's necessary. Suppose I paint an apple and you ask me what it means. Well, I don't know what it means either, because the meaning is not important. It carries an innate meaning with it, so it already has a meaning. That's the way it is with artworks: you have to relax. I reduce or completely get rid of the artwork's correspondence to reality. I feel it's not necessary at all. I feel that with superior artworks, it is a matter of the artist's fantasy. It is not a mater of faithfulness. The rousing thing about it is something else, some feeling the viewer gets when looking at it. At that moment, there is no need of anything else. After I finished grad school, I taught at the university for a few years, but later I gave up teaching. It was upsetting, because at first I was idealistic and wanted to teach the classes well. Later I discovered this would be impossible. Because of the way the system was set up, it was impossible for one's teaching to turn out well. Even what you thought was a good approach would soon be countermanded and turned into something else. I feel that we don't have much choice; one doesn't really have any choice. In truth the idea of having a choice is a deception. Not having a choice is the answer. When you feel there is a choice, I feel that you have a problem. We are all in a perplexed state.

Pi San /

That's right. I see that recently you have done paintings of books. It is intriguing. I had a period when I really liked to paint books. People around me said I thought I was some kind of intellectual.

/ Guan Yong

As soon as books come up, they are connected to intellectuals. When I started painting them it wasn't that way at all. I was painting my own bookcase. I was just interested in the vertical and horizontal lines that were made by putting books on a shelf. That was what I wanted to paint.

Pi San /

My bookcase is a lot like yours. I feel that on a deeper level, each has habits that the other can identify with.

[1] The four famous traditional novels of China are Dream of Red Mansions by Cao Xueqing, Romance of Three Kingdoms by Luo Guanzhong, Along the Water Margin by Shi Naian, and Journey to the West by Wu Cheng'en.

白门秋柳　2009年　布面油彩　200cm × 150cm

Nanjing Autumn Willow　2009　oil on canvas　200cm×150cm

沉思录　2011年　布面油彩　180cm × 220cm

Meditations　2011　oil on canvas　180cm×220cm

S先生的阅读　2011年　布面油彩　80cm × 60cm

Mr. S's Reading　2011　oil on canvas　80cm×60cm

飘动的红　2011年　布面油彩　80cm × 60cm

Drifting Red　2011　oil on canvas　80cm×60cm

策展人及艺术家简历

Resumes of Curator and Artists

策展人
The Curator

006

[杭春晓]

1976年出生，安徽当涂人。2002年毕业于南京艺术学院，获美术史硕士学位。2006年毕业于中国艺术研究院，获美术史博士学位。现为中国艺术研究院美术研究所副研究员。先后在学术期刊发表《商周青铜器饕餮纹研究述评》、《绘画资源的开放——古物陈列所与民初中国画》、《重读蔡元培"实物写生"论》、《认知眼光与二十世纪中国画》、《文人理想的幻灭与重建——文徵明的出仕、致仕及其心理辨析》等论文数篇；出版《中国美术考古学史纲》、《明代吴门画派》、《商周青铜器之饕餮纹研究》；参与编著高校教材《中国美术史》、《中国古代绘画史》；独立承担国家课题"民初美术改良之价值重审"；组织策划过"新改良——新锐画展"、"幻象·本质——中国工笔画当代性探索展"、"楼上的青年——2010青年批评家提名展"、"思想 > 手感"等展览及活动。

[Hang chunxiao]

Born 1976 in Dangtu, Anhui, graduated 2002 from Nanjing Art Institute with M.A. in Art History, is now Associate professor at China Art Research Institute. Has published the following articles in scholarly journals: "A Study of Taotie Patterns on Shang and Zhou Bronzes," "Opening Up Painting Resources: The Ancient Relic Display Center and Paintings of the Early Republican Period," "A New Reading of Cai Yuanpei's 'Painting from Life with Concrete Subjects,'" "Cognitive Insights and 20th Century Chinese Art," "Disillusionment and Reconstruction of Literati Ideals: A Psychological Inquiry into Wen Zhenghui's Official Career." His published books include Outline History of Fine Arts Archaeology in China, History of Ancient Chinese Painting, The Ming Dynasty Wu School of Painting. Has independently undertaken a national research project: "Revaluation of Fine Arts Amelioration in the Early Republican Period." He has curated such exhibits as "New Amelioration—Pathbreaking Painters"; "Ilusion and Essence—Explorations of Contemporaneity in Chinese Fine-Brush Ink Painting"; "Thinking > Tactile Sense."

艺术家（按姓氏笔画排序）
The Artists

(The order according to the number of strokes of the first Chinese characters of each name)

025

[王光乐]

1976　出生于福建
2000　毕业于中央美术学院油画系
现居住于北京

个展

2011
"王光乐"，北京公社，北京，中国

2009
"王光乐"，北京公社，北京，中国

2007
"寿漆"，aye 画廊，北京，中国

2005
"汉语"，一月当代画廊，北京，中国

群展

2011
"箭厂窟：掉队小组"，箭厂空间，北京，中国
"艺术长沙：解离"，湖南省博物馆，长沙，中国
"白相"，J 空间，上海，中国
"群像"，东站画廊 北京，中国
"手感 4"，视界艺术中心，上海，中国
"飞越对流层：新一代绘画备忘录"，伊比利亚艺术中心，北京，中国
"慢艺术：中国抽象"，拉伦辛格博物馆，荷兰
"绘画课——错觉或幻象"，杨画廊，北京，中国
"摆摊 3：抽——年青艺术家匿名展"，西五画廊，北京，中国
"十年白兔"，白兔美术馆，悉尼，澳大利亚
"视觉结构"，A4 艺术中心，成都，中国

2010
"北京之声：在一起或孤芳自赏"，佩斯画廊，北京，中国
"控"，5 楼艺术中心，广州，中国
"视觉运动——架上绘画研究展之一：空间与能量"，青和美术馆，南京，中国
"同化古典——中国当代抽象绘画中的空间深度"，元典美术馆，北京，中国
"掉队 5"，西五画廊，北京，中国
"调节器——第二届今日文献展"，今日美术馆，北京，中国
"地点：龙泉洗浴"，草场地龙泉洗浴，北京，中国
"自驾游——掉队小组"，器．Haus 空间，重庆，中国
"釜山双年展"，釜山文化中心，韩国
"次声计划第二回展——一而二，二而一"，纯粹当代艺术空间，北京，中国
"是与否 / 一个似另一个 / 特殊的笔画"，黑桥 OFF 空间，北京，中国
"楼上青年"，时代美术馆，北京，中国
"改造历史 2000——2009 年的中国新艺术"，国家会议中心，北京，中国
"中国当代艺术三十年历程"，民生现代美术馆，上海，中国
"摆摊——表态"，西五画廊，北京，中国
"七个年青艺术家"，北京公社，北京，中国
"丛林——中国当代艺术生态管窥"，站台中国，北京，中国

2009
"工作坊：艺术家是如何工作的"，伊比利亚艺术中心，北京，中国
"空白展·制造生活"，中间艺术馆，北京，中国
"场"，大象艺术空间馆，台中，中国
"再实验：智性与意志的重申——青年艺术家推荐展"，798 金属库，北京，中国
"摆摊"，尚堡美术馆，北京，中国
"时间的能量"，昌 art，北京，中国
"在——抽象绘画"，偏锋画廊，北京，中国
"文本：活在当下的中国绘画"，荔空间，北京，中国
"第四届布拉格双年展"，布拉格卡林厅，捷克共和国
"回望中国"，东站画廊，北京，中国

2008
"独白：艺术的重建"，水木当代，北京，中国
"BCA 艺术市集"，天安时间，北京，中国
"物是"，玛吉画廊，北京，中国
"演变"，路德维希美术馆，科布伦茨，德国
"梦蝶"，上海当代艺术馆，上海，中国
"找自己"，上海民生当代艺术中心，上海，中国
"观念的笔记：中国当代绘画的局部叙述"，伊比利亚当代艺术中心，北京，中国
"走向后抽象"，偏锋画廊，北京，中国
"学院与非学院 Ⅱ"，艺博画廊，上海，中国
"七零后艺术档案"，别处空间，北京，中国
"新界面 4"，红桥画廊，上海，中国
"柳暗花明——当代艺术中的后传统现象"，空白空间，北京，中国

2007
"刷新"，上海证大美术馆，上海；阿拉里奥画廊，北京，中国
"新界面 3"，刘海粟美术馆；红桥画廊，上海，中国
"抽象叙事"，北京德山艺术空间，北京，中国
"空白展"，上海可当代艺术中心，上海，中国

2006
“形无形——中国抽象绘画展”，一月当代画廊，北京，中国
“N12——第四回展”，西五画廊，北京，中国
“画幅决定态度”首届 5×7(平遥)照相双年展，平遥，山西；北京 TS1 当代艺术中心，北京，中国
“新界面”，刘海粟美术馆，上海，中国
“虚虚实实”,HEYRI 艺术基金会文化空间，首尔，韩国
“冷能”，北京表画廊，北京，中国

2005
“坏孩子天空”，星空间画廊，北京，中国
“翻手为云覆手为雨”，TS1 当代艺术中心，北京，中国
“N12——第三回展”，中央美院美术馆，北京，中国

2004
“N12——第二回展”，中央美院美术馆，北京，中国
“少年心气——中国新锐绘画奖”，何香凝美术馆，深圳，中国

2003
“N12——第一回展”，中央美院美术馆，北京，中国
“第三届全国油画展”，中国美术馆，北京，中国
“念珠与笔触”，东京画廊，北京，中国

2000
“二厂时代”，云峰画苑，北京，中国

[Wang Guangle]

1976 Born in Songxi, Fujian
2000 Graduated from Oil Painting Department, Central Academy of Fine Arts, Beijing, China
Current: Lives in Beijing, China

Solo Exhibitions

2011
"Wang Guangle", Beijing Commune, Beijing, China

2009
"Wang Guangle", Beijing Commune, Beijing, China

2007
"Coffin Paint", Aye gallery, Beijing, China

2005
"Waterstone", Onemoon Gallery, Beijing, China

Group Exhibitions

2011
"Arrow Factory Grotto - Diao Dui Collective", Arrow factory, Beijing, China
"Art Changsha 2011: Dissociation", Hunan Provincial Museum, Hunan, China
"Nothing White", J Gallery, Shanghai, China
"Portraits", Eastation Gallery, Beijing, China
"Hands on No.4", V Art Center, Shanghai, China
"Fly through the Troposphere: Memo of the New Generation Painting", Iberia Center for Contemporary Art, Beijing, China
"Chinese Abstract 'Slow' Art", Singer Museum in Laren, The Netherlands
"Panting Lesson I: Illusion or Delusion", Yang Gallery, Beijing, China
"Extract: The 3rd Stall Keeper Show", C5 Art, Beijing, China
"Decade of the Rabbit", White Rabbit Art Museum, Sydney, Australia
"Visual Structure", A4 CAC, Chengdu, China

2010
"Beijing Voice: Together or Isolated", Pace Beijing, Beijing, China
"Con", 5 Art Space ,Guangzhou,China
"Visual Flux - Easel Painting Research Exhibition I: Space and Energy", Nanjing Qinghe Current Art Center , Nanjing, China
"Assimilating Antiquity: Depth in Space in Contemporary Abstract Chinese Painting", Beijing Yuan Art Museum, Beijing, China
"Diao dui 5", C5 Art, Beijing, China
"Negotiation--the Second Today's Documents", Today Art Museum, Beijing, China
"Location: Dragon Fountain Bathhouse", Caochangdi Dragon Fountain Bathhouse, Beijing, China
"Busan Biennale", Busan Cultural Center, Busan, Korea
"Self-driving Tour: Diao Dui Collective ", Organhaus, Chongqing, China
"The 2nd Infrasound Plan: One but Two, Two but One", Chuncui Art Space, Beijing, China
"Yes and No/One is like the other - spacial strokes", Blackbridge Offspace, Beijing, China
"Reshaping History: Chinart from 2000 to2009", China National Convention Center, Beijing, China
"Thirty Year Journey of Chinese Contemporary Art", Minsheng Art Museum,Shanghai, China
"Commit - the 2nd Stall Keeper Show", C5 Art, Beijing, China
"Seven Young Artists", Beijing Commune, Beijing, China
"Jungle - A Close-up Focus on Chinese Contemporary Art Trends", Platform China, Beijing, China

2009
"Work in Progress: How Do Artists Work?", Iberia Center for Contemporary Art, Beijing, China
"Blank3: Making Life", Medium Art Center, Beijing, China
"Chang", Daxiang Art Space, Taizhong, Taiwan, China
"Re-experimentation: a Reaffirmation of Will and Enlightenment"-Young Artists Promotional Exhibition, 798 Originality Square Metal Warehouse, Beijing, China
"Stall", Shangpu Art Museum, Beijing, China
"Energy of Time", Chang Art, Beijing, China
"Where the Spirit Lives", PIFO New Art Studio, Beijing, China
"Textbook: an Exhibition of Lively Chinese Paintings", Li Space, Beijing, China
"Prague Biennale 4 ", Prague, Czech
"China's Revision - Focus Beijing", Eastation Gallery, Beijing, China

2008
"Soliloquy: the Reconstruction of Art", Shui Mu Contemporary Art Space, Beijing, China
"The Market: New Year Gifts From 60 Young Artists", Beijing Center for the Arts at Legation Quarter, Beijing, China
"Thinghood: Object - Related Thesis in Contemporary Art", Magee Art Gallery, Beijing, China
"China's Revision - Focusing Beijing", Museum Ludwig, Koblenz, Germany
"Butterfly Dream", Zendai Museum of Modern of Art, Shanghai, China
"Looking for Me", Minsheng Center for Contemporary Art, Shanghai, China
"Notes of Conception: A Local Narrative of Chinese Contemporary Painting", Iberia Center for Contemporary Art, Beijing, China
"Toward the Post-abstract", PIFO New Art Studio, Beijing, China
"The third A+A", PIFO New Art Studio, Beijing, China
"Acdemic and Un-acdemic Ⅱ ", Yibo Gallery, Shanghai, China
"Blank2: Begin with the Beginning", Medium Art Center, Beijing, China
"Post '70s Art Archives", Beyond Art Space, Beijing, China
"New Interface IV", H&H Space, Shanghai, China
"New Vista:The Phenomenon of Post-Tradition in Contemporary Art", Whitespace, Beijing, China

2007
"Refresh - Emerging Chinese Artist", Zendai

Museum of Modern Art, Shanghai; Arario, Beijing, China
"New Interface 3", Liu Haisu Art Museum; H&H space, Shanghai, China
"Abstract and Narratability", Y.Q.K Art Space, Beijing, China
"Blank", Ke Center, Shanghai, China

2006
"Visible/invisible: Abstract Art of China", Onemoon Gallery, Beijing, China
"N12" No. 4, C5 Art Gallery, Beijing, China
"Size Decide Manner", The First Biennale of 5×7" Photo (Pingyao), Pingyao, Shanxi; TS1 Art Center, Beijing, China
"New Interface - Landing of Up Generation", Liu Haisu Art Museum, Shanghai, China
"Unclear and Clear", Heyri Foundation, Seoul, Korea
"Cold Energy", PYO Gallery, Beijing, China

2005
"Naughty Kids - the Chinese New Generation Born after the 1970", Start Gallery, Beijing, China
"Sleight of Mind", TS1 Art Center, Beijing, China
"N12"No.3, Art Museum of Central Academy of Fine Arts, Beijing, China

2004
"N12" No.2, Art Museum of Central Academy of Fine Arts, Beijing, China
"Ideal of New Generation - Chinese New Generatin Artist Award exhibition", He Xiangning Art Museum,Shenzhen, China

2003
"N12" No.1, Art Museum of Central Academy of Fine Arts, Beijing, China
"The Third Exhibition of Chinese Oil Paintings", National Art Museum, Beijing, China
"Prayer Beads and Brush Strokes", Beijing Tokyo Art Projects, Beijing

2000
"The Second Factory Time", YunFeng Gallery, Beijing, China

043

[王 颉]

1978 生于天津
1998 毕业于中央美术学院附中
2002 毕业于中央美术学院油画系 获学士学位
2008 毕业于中央美术学院油画系 获硕士学位

个展
2010
"虚空妙有"，杰・艺术画廊，上海，中国
2008
"虚迷"，新时代画廊，北京，中国

群展
2011
台北国际艺术博览会，台湾，中国
"70，80 多元世代 PART 23 —— 辨・变・辩"，新时代画廊，北京，中国
"过去，现在，未来—— 新时代 20 年回顾"，新时代画廊，台湾，中国

2010
台北国际艺术博览会，台湾，中国
"美学的多样性：世界美学大会邀请展"，北京大学，中国
"年轻力量：艺术北京邀请展"，环铁时代美术馆，北京，中国
中国国际画廊博览会，北京，中国

2009
"返身三次方"，夸克艺术空间，北京，中国
"原点"，鼎美术馆，北京，中国
中国国际画廊博览会，北京，中国

2008
"全国艺术硕士研究生优秀作品展"，中国美术馆，北京，中国
"回声"，中央美术学院美术馆，北京，中国
新加坡国际艺术博览会，新加坡
"未来天空：中国当代青年艺术家提名展"，今日美术馆，北京，中国
"新时代・新交融：中国＼印尼新一代艺术家交流展"，新时代画廊，北京，中国；Edwin's Gallery，雅加达，印度尼西亚
"创新世代・各执己见"，新时代画廊；中国国际画廊博览会，北京，中国
"生命看见"，中央美术学院美术馆，北京，中国

2007
"时光中的时光：新锐艺术家展"，夸克艺术空间，北京，中国
"酸酸甜甜的一代"，曼海姆美术馆，柏林，德国
"上海艺术博览会国际当代艺术展"，上海国际展览中心，上海，中国
"新时代・异宣言"，中国国际画廊博览会，北京，中国
"多元世代・固执己见"，新时代画廊，北京；台湾，中国

2006
"当代油画邀请展"，中外博艺画廊，北京，中国
"N12——绘画第四回展"，西五画廊，北京，中国
"解构童话的力量"，夸克艺术空间，北京，中国

2005
"N12——绘画第三回展"，中央美术学院王府井陈列馆，北京，中国

2004
"N12——绘画第二回展"，中央美术学院王府井陈列馆，北京，中国
"当代・学院・艺术"邀请展，三合艺术中心，北京，中国
"个性・魅力"青年艺术邀请展，三合艺术中心，北京，中国

2003
"N12——绘画第一回展"，中央美术学院王府井陈列馆，北京，中国

2001
"向后退"，当代美术馆，北京，中国

2000
"二厂时代"提名展，云峰画苑，北京，中国

[Wang Jie]

1978 Born in Tianjin
1998 Graduated from the Affiliated High School of Central Academy of Fine Arts
2002 Graduated from the Oil Painting Department of Central Academy of Fine Arts. BFA.
2008 Graduated from the Oil Painting Department of Central Academy of Fine Arts. MFA.

Solo Exhibitions
2010
Emptiness and Existence, J Art Gallery, Shanghai, China

2008
Lost in the Shade, New Age Gallery, Beijing, China

Selected Group Exhibitions
2011
ART Taipei 2011, Taiwan, China
The Age of Pluralism Part 23 – Distinguish·Transform·Dialectic, New Age Gallery, Beijing, China
"Past, Present, Future": Twenty-year Review of New Age Gallery, Taiwan, China

2010
ART Taipei 2010, Taiwan, China
Diversities in Aesthetics: Invitation Art Exhibition Gala of the Eighteenth International Congress

of Aesthetics, Peking University, China
Youth Power: Art Beijing Invitation Exhibition, Huantie Tines Art Museum, Beijing, China.
China International Gallery Exposition(CIGE), Beijing, China

2009

Returning Cube, Quac Art Space, Beijing, China
Origin, Ding Museum, Beijing, China
China International Gallery Exposition(CIGE), Beijing, China

2008

China MFA Excellent Works Exhibition, National Art Museum of China, Beijing, China
Echo, Art Museum of Central Academy of Fine Arts, Beijing, China
Art Singapore2008: The Contemporary Asian Art Fair, Suntec, Singapore
Future Sky: Chinese Contemporary Young Artists Works Selection Exhibition, Today Art Museum, Beijing, China
"New Age, New Blending": New Generation Chinese and Indonesian Artists Exchange Exhibition, New Age Gallery, Beijing, China; Edwin's Gallery, Jakarta, Indonesia
"The Age of Innovation, Being persistent", New Age Gallery, Beijing, China
"The Age of Innovation, Being persistent", China International Gallery Exposition, Beijing, China
See Life, Art Museum of Central Academy of Fine Arts, Beijing, China

2007

High Light in the Era: Artists Exhibition, Quac Art Space, Beijing, China.
Joys and Sorrows in Generation, Mannheim Art Museum, Berlin, Germany
Shanghai Art Fair International Contemporary Art Exhibition, INTEx Shanghai, China
"New Age, Different Manifesto", China International Gallery Exposition, Beijing, China
"The Age of Pluralism, Being Persistent", New Age Gallery, Beijing\Taiwan, China

2006

An Invitational Contemporary Oil Painting Exhibition, Zhongwai Boyi Gallery, Beijing, China
"N12" the Forth Exhibition, C5 Art Gallery, Beijing, China
The Power of Disassemble Fairy Tale, Quac Art Space, Beijing, China

2005

"N12" the Third Exhibition, Wangfujing Art Museum of Central Academy of Fine Arts, Beijing, China

2004

"N12" the Second Exhibition, Wangfujing Art Museum of Central Academy of Fine Arts, Beijing, China
"Contemporary, Academy and Art" Nomination Exhibition, San He Art Center, Beijing, China
Individuality and Enchantment: an Contemporary Chinese New Artists Nomination Exhibition, San He Art Center, Beijing, China

2003

"N12" Art Exhibition, Wangfujing Art Museum of Central Academy of Fine Arts, Beijing, China

2001

Backward, Contemporary Museum, Beijing, China

2000

"Er Chang Times" Nomination Exhibition, Wan Fung Art Gallery, Beijing, China

061

[尹朝阳]

1970 生于河南省南阳市
1996 毕业于中央美术学院版画系
1996 ~ 职业艺术家，现居北京

个展

2011

“空山夕照”，林舍画廊，台北大未来，中国
“石窟”，亦安画廊，北京，中国
“朝圣”，亦安画廊，香港，中国

2010

“四季岛”，唐人画廊，香港，中国
“正面”，广东美术馆，广东，中国
“巨匠”，民生银行美术馆，上海，中国
“正面”，上海美术馆，上海，中国
“正面”，伊比利亚当代艺术中心，北京，中国

2009

“入寺显佛”，嵩山少林寺，河南，中国

2008

“尹朝阳——十年”，民生艺术中心，上海，中国
“辐射”，洛杉矶，美国；DF2 画廊，中国
“尹朝阳 1997——2007”，今日美术馆，北京，中国
“焦点”，唐人画廊，香港，中国

2007

“台北日记”，亚洲艺术中心，台湾，中国
“尹朝阳新作展”，唐人画廊，北京，中国
“流动”，泰康顶层空间，北京，中国
“尹朝阳近作展”，亦安画廊，香港，中国
“经过・毛泽东”，DF2 画廊，洛杉矶，美国

2006

“经过・毛泽东”，环碧堂画廊，北京，中国
“经过・毛泽东”，唐人画廊，曼谷，泰国
“神话”，今日美术馆，北京；亦安画廊，上海，中国

2005

“公共空间”，Max Protetch 画廊，纽约，美国
“青春・乌托邦”，唐人画廊，曼谷，泰国

2004

“乌托邦”，中央美术学院美术馆，北京，中国
“乌托邦 vs 青春物语”，多伦现代美术馆，上海，中国

2002

“神话”，亦安画廊，上海，中国

2001

“神话”，北京艺术博物馆，北京，中国

群展

2011

“狠・现实”，银石空间，上海，中国

2010

“光州艺术博览会”，光州，韩国
“one and one 时代青年艺术家第一回展——语言”，北京，时代美术馆，中国
“图像消费”，时代美术馆，北京，中国
“趣味的共同体”，智利当代美术馆，智利
“楼上的青年”，时代美术馆，北京，中国
“时代画农民”，浙江美术馆，杭州，中国

2009

“反光——新艺术的纵深”，西湖美术馆，杭州；墙美术馆，北京，中国
“北京哈瓦那中国当代艺术展”，古巴国家美术馆，哈瓦那，古巴

2008

“北京雅典中国当代艺术展”，希腊国家美术馆，希腊
“第三届南京三年展”，南视觉美术馆，南京，中国
“个案——艺术史和艺术批评中的艺术家”，圣之空间艺术中心，北京，中国
“画纸藏龙”，F2 画廊，北京，中国
“五谷杂粮 UNPACK——中国实验艺术教育与创作展”，中国美术学院，杭州，中国
“二十一世纪的中国——处在个人身份与社会转型之间的当代艺”，罗马，意大利

2007

“截点·当代艺术的中国形象”，三峡博物馆，重庆，中国

“天行健——中国当代艺术的前沿”，亚洲艺术中心，北京，中国

“黑白灰——一种主动的文化选择”，今日美术馆，北京，中国

“金蝉脱壳——从传统和革命中的语言拯救”，四方当代美术馆，南京，中国

“新地标——上海 800 号美术馆首展”，上海 800 号美术馆，上海，中国

“七座高原——当代艺术展”，名谷艺术画廊，北京，中国

“韩·中现代美术展——幻影中的巨人”，首尔市立美术馆，韩国

“中国当代社会艺术展”，特列恰可夫国家美术馆，莫斯科，俄罗斯

2006

“展开的现实主义——1978 年以来中国大陆油画”，台北市立美术馆，台湾，中国

“幻想与前景——中国当代艺术展”，马尼拉大都会博物馆，菲律宾

“超验的中国”，阿拉里奥，北京艺术空间，北京，中国

2005

“70 后艺术”，刘海粟现代美术馆，上海；今日美术馆，北京，中国

“中国艺术三年展”，南京博物院，中国

“麻将——希克收藏展”，瑞士

2003

“图像的图像”，深圳美术馆，中国

2002

“青春残酷绘画”，东大名艺术创库，上海；炎黄艺术馆，北京，中国

2001

“第一届成都双年展”，成都现代艺术馆，中国

1999

“新锐的目光”，国际艺苑美术馆，北京，中国

[Yin Chaoyang]

1970 Born in Nanyang, Henan, China

1996 Graduated from the Printing Department, Central Academy of Fine Arts, Beijing, China

Lives and works in Beijing

Solo Exhibitions

2011

Cave – Yin Chaoyang Solo Exhibition, Aura Gallery, Beijing, China

Pilgrim– Yin Chaoyang Solo Exhibition, Aura Gallery, Hongkong, China

2010

The Four Seasons Island , Tang Contemporary, HongKong, China

Master, Minsheng Bank Art Museum, Shanghai, China

Facade,Iberia Center for Contemporary Art, Beijing, China

2009

Enter the Temple and Buddha Appears, Shaolin Temple in Henan Songshan

2008

Radiation, DF2 Gallery, Los Angeles, USA

Yin Chaoyang 1997—2007, Today Art Museum, Beijing, China

Focus, Tang Gallery, Hong Kong, China

2007

Taipei Journal, Asia Art Center, Taiwan, China

Yin Chaoyang's New Work,Tang Contemporary Art, Beijing, China

Time Lapse,Taikang Top Space, Beijing, China

Yin Chaoyang's Recent Work, Aura Gallery, Hong Kong, China

Passing By Mao Zedong, DF2 Gallery, Los Angeles, USA

The Twilight of A Man, ARCO Madrid, Spain

2006

Passing By Mao Zedong, China Blue Gallery, Beijing, China

Passing By Mao Zedong, Tang Gallery Bangkok, Thailand

Mythology, Today Art Museum, Beijing, China

Mythology, Aura Gallery, Shanghai, China

2005

Youth·Utopia, Tang Gallery Bangkok, Thailand

Public Space, Max Protetch Gallery, New York, USA

2004

Utopia, Museum of Central Academy of Fine Art, Beijing, China

Utopia vs. Young Story, Duolun Museum of Modern Art, Shanghai, China

2002

Mythology, Aura Gallery, Shanghai, China

2001

Mythology, Beijing Art Museum, Beijing, China

Selected Group Exhibitions

2011

Ruthless Reality, White Stone Space, Shanghai, China

2010

Art Guangju 2010 , Guangju, Korea

"One and One" Age Young Artists for the First Time Image Consumption, Times Art Museum, Beijing, China

Community of Tastes Chile Contemporary Art Museum, Chile

The Upstairs Youth, Times Art Museum, Beijing, China

Time Painting Farmers, Zhejiang Museum, Hangzhou, China

2009

Glisten - New Art in Depth, Hangzhou West lake Art Museum, Zhejiang; Wall Art Museum, Beijing, China

Beijing-Havana Chinese contemporary Exhibition, National Art Museum of Cuba, Havana, Cuba

Beijing-Havana Chinese Contemporary Exhibition, Cuba Contry Art Museum, Havana

2008

Case Studies of Artists in Art History and Art Criticism, SZ Art Center of Fine Arts Publishing House, Beijing, China

Crouching Paper, Hidden Dragon, F2 Gallery, Beijing, China

China 21 Century: Art Between Identity and Transformation, Palaexpo Delle Esposizioni, Rome, Italy

2007

Section– Chinese Image of Contemporary Art, 3G Museum, Chongqing, China

Exhibition of Frontier Contemporary Chinese Art, Asia Art Center, Beijing, China

Black White Grey- A Conscious Cultural Stance, Today Art Museum, Beijing, China

Escape By Scheme Salvation from Traditional and Revolution Language, Square Gallery of Contemporary Art, Nanjing, China

New Terrestrial Reference- Opening of Art Museum 800, Art Museum 800, Shanghai, China

Seven Plateaus– Contemporary Art, Ming Art Gallery, Beijing, China

Korean & Chinese Modern Art Exhibition: Giants in Illusion, Seoul, Korea

Chinese Contemporary SOCART, The State Tretyakov Gallery, Moscow, Russia

2006

The Blossoming of Realism- The Oil Painting of Mainland China since 1978, Taipei Fine Arts Museum, Taiwan, China
Future and Fantasy- An Exhibition of Contemporary Art, The Metropolitan of Manila, Philippines
Beyond Experience New China, Arario Gallery, Beijing, China

2005
Artists Born after the 70's, Liu Haisu Art Museum, Shanghai, China
Artists Born after the 70's, Today Art Museum, Beijing, China
The Second Triennial of Chinese Art, Nanjing Museum, China
Mahjong- Sigg Collection Exhibition, Switzerland

2003
Image about Images, Shenzhen Art Museum, Shenzhen, China

2002
The Youth Cruelty Painting, DdM Art Warehouse, Shanghai, China
The Youth Cruelty Painting, Yanhuang Art Museum, Beijing, China

2001
First Chengdu Biennale, Chengdu Modern Art Museum, Chengdu, China

1999
Sharp New Sights, Beijing International Art Museum, Beijing, China

077

[李 晖]

1977 生于中国北京
2003 毕业于中央美术学院，中国北京
现工作、居住于中国北京

个展
2011
“不确定的真相”，台北当代艺术馆，台北，台湾，中国
“V”，尤伦斯当代艺术中心，北京，中国
“笼子”，Ernst Schering 基金会，柏林，德国

2010
“游离——李晖”，曼海姆艺术协会，曼海姆，德国
“不可预期的……”，当代唐人艺术中心，北京，中国
“谁害怕红色，琥珀和绿色？”，光美术馆，埃因霍恩，荷兰
“机械的仪式”，宗德耀美术馆，雅加达，印尼

2009
“维度之间——李晖个展”，关渡美术馆，台北，台湾，中国
“李晖——虚与实的物性”，当代唐人艺术中心，香港，中国
“入口——李晖个展”，北京现在画廊，北京，中国

2008
“闪亮——李晖 A Art Contemporary Space ”，台北，台湾，中国
“灭渡——李晖个展”，外滩 18 号创意中心，上海，中国

2007
“Spin”，当代唐人艺术中心，北京，中国

群展
2011
“自选动作”，荔空间，北京，中国
“过去·现在·未来”，新时代画廊，台中，台湾，中国
“复感·动观——2011 海峡两岸当代艺术展”，中国美术馆，北京，中国
“复感·动观——2011 海峡两岸当代艺术展”，台湾美术馆，台中，台湾，中国
"Matière-Lumière Matter-Light"，Béthune 2011 Capitale Régionale de la Culture Béthune，法国
"CAR CULTURE. Medien der Mobilität"， ZKM Karlsruhe，德国
“未来通行证——2011 年威尼斯双年展平行专题展”，克劳迪欧布几奥基金会，威尼斯，意大利
“延展生命：媒体中国 2011——国际新媒体艺术三年展”，中国美术馆，北京，中国
《大周末 Hotspot》四周年庆暨首届“城市趣味”明星名人当代艺术推荐收藏展，今日美术馆，北京，中国
“破晓”，阿拉里奥画廊，北京，中国
“破晓”，阿拉里奥画廊，天安，韩国
“龙生九子——隋建国师生作品展”，红星画廊，北京，中国
“清晰的地平线——1978 以来的中国当代雕塑展”，寺上美术馆，北京，中国
“70s 菁锐进行式”，大未来林舍画廊，台北，台湾，中国

2010
“亚洲路标：丰田艺术项目”，伊比利亚当代艺术中心，北京，中国
“滤窗——中国年轻艺术家群展”，别处空间，北京，中国
“云端——亚洲当代艺术大展”，北京索卡艺术中心，北京，中国
“东方 / 西方：视觉谈话”，MOCA Jacksonville 杰克·逊维尔，佛罗里达州，美国
“往返 北京——纽约现在多姆斯收藏精选”，尤伦斯当代艺术中心，北京，中国
“调节器——第二届今日文献展”，偏锋艺术空间，北京，中国
“陷阱”，艺术 ISSUE Projects，北京，中国
“超时尚——中国年轻艺术家时装设计师跨界展第一回”，别处空间，北京，中国
"Internationale Lichttage Winterthur 2010"，Winterthur，Switzerland
“趣味的共同体：2000 年以来的中国当代艺术”，智利当代美术馆，智利

2009
“欢迎光临”，百艺画廊，台北，台湾，中国
Art in Busan 2009 Inter-City，釜山市立现代美术馆，釜山，韩国
“白盒子艺术馆开幕暨‘主场’当代艺术展”，白盒子艺术馆，北京，中国

2008
“面对现实”，中国美术馆，北京，中国
“2008 意大利威尼斯国际雕塑装置展 (OPEN 2008)”，意大利威尼斯丽都岛，威尼斯，意大利
“开启与扩张——第 5 届首尔国际媒体艺术双年展”，首尔市立美术馆，首尔，韩国
“艺术的魅力——中国当代艺术及收藏展”，今日美术馆，北京，中国

2007
EXIT 艺术节，Maison des Arts 美术馆，巴黎，法国
VIA 艺术节，Manège 美术馆，法国 Maubeuge
“亦真亦幻”，望东艺集，上海，中国
“温存——关于记忆的十二种绘本”，北京帝门艺术中心，北京，中国
大山子艺术节主题展，北京大山子 798，北京，中国
“有界，无界”，上海新天地，上海，中国
琴山画廊开幕展，北京环铁艺术区，北京，中国
“浮游——中国美术新趋势”，韩国国立现代美术馆，首尔，韩国
“中国：面对现实”，路德维希基金会当代美术馆，维也纳，奥地利
“透视的景观”，深圳何香凝美术馆，深圳，中国

2006
韩国釜山双年展，Naru 公园，釜山，韩国
“冷能”，表画廊，北京，中国
“中国制造”，公共场所，柏林，德国
上海双年展，上海美术馆，上海，中国
中国当代艺术节 2006，Heyriyi 艺术村，首尔，韩国
“二踢脚”，北京当代唐人艺术中心，北京，中国
亚洲当代艺术，Loop 艺术中心，首尔，韩国
“自由行”，Osage 画廊，香港，中国
大众汽车中国玛卡现代艺术展——移动的艺术，北京东方广场，北京，中国

2005
“透明的盒子”，建外 SOHO，北京，中国

成都双年展，成都现代艺术馆，北京，中国
“一万年前”，后现代城，北京，中国
“虚拟的爱”，上海当代美术馆，上海，中国
“一界两端——当代艺术中的设计呈现”，深圳何香凝美术馆，深圳，中国

2004
“游于气”，资生堂画廊，东京，日本

2003
“雕塑作品展”，东京画廊，北京，中国
后现代城《漂流记》，后现代城，北京，中国
北京双年展外围展《雌雄同体》，798 艺术西区，北京，中国

2002
“国际城市雕塑艺术展”，北京雕塑公园，北京，中国

[Li Hui]

1977 Born in Beijing
2003 Graduated from the Central Academy of Fine Arts,Beijing, China
Currently lives and works in Beijing, China

Solo Exhibitions

2011
"Reality Impalpable," Taipei Museum of Contemporary Art, Taipei, Taiwan, China
"V", Ullens Center For Contemporary Art, Beijing, China
"Cage", Ernst Schering Foundation, Birlin, Germany

2010
"Transition—Li Hui", Mannheimer Kunstverein Mannheim, Germany
"Unexpected…", Tang Contemporary Art—Beijing, Beijing, China
"Who's Afraid of Red, Amber and Green? ", Light Art Museum, Eindhoven, The Netherlands
"Gadgetry and Rites", Yuz Museum, Jakarta, Indonesia

2009
"Between Dimensions – Li Hui Solo Exhibition", Kuandu Museum of Fine Arts, Taipei, Taiwan, China
"Dialectics of Void & Substance", Tang Contemporary Art ---Hong Kong, Hong Kong, China
"Entrance—Li Hui Solo Exhibition", Beijing Art Now Gallery, Beijing, China

2008
"Shiny Li Hui" , A Art Contemporary Space, Taipei, Taiwan, China
"Samsara-Li Hui Solo Exhibition", Bund18 Creative Center.SH, Shanghai, China

2007
"Spin" , Tang Contemporary Art Centre, Beijing, China

Group Exhibitions

2011
"Optional Exercise", Li Space, Beijing, China
"Past/Present/Future", New Age Gallery, Taichung, Taiwan, China
"Dual Senses and Dynamic Views-Contemporary Art Exhibition across the Taiwan Straits of 2011", National Art Museum of China, Beijing, China
"Dual Senses and Dynamic Views-Contemporary Art Exhibition across the Taiwan Straits of 2011", National Taiwan Museum of Fine Arts, Taizhong, Taiwan, China
"Matière-Lumière Matter-Light", Béthune 2011 Capitale Régionale de la Culture, Béthune, France
"Car Culture. Medien der Mobilität" , ZKM Karlsruhe, Germany
"Future Pass-Collateral Event of the 54th Venice Biennial", Fondazione Claudio Buziol Introduction, Venice, Italy
"Translife: Media Art China 2011—International Tiennial of New Media Art", National Art Museum of China, Beijing, China
"The Future is Already Here", Today Art Museum, Beijing, China
"Daybreak", Arario Gallery, Beijing, China
"Daybreak",Arario Gallery Cheonan, Korea
"Endless Variations" ,Red Star Gallery, Beijing, China
"Start From the Horizon-Chinese Contemporary Sculpture since 1978", Si Shang Art Museum, Beijing, China
"Born in the 70s", Lin & Lin Gallery, Taipei, Taiwan, China

2010
"Asian Landmark; Toyota Art Project", Iberia Center for Contemporary Art, Beijing, China
"Filter Window—Young Chinese Artists Group Exhibition", Beyond Art Space, Beijing, China
"Clouds: Power of Asian Contemporary Art", Soka Art Center, Beijing, China
"East/West: Visually Speaking", Museum of Contemporary Art Jacksonville, Jacksonville, FL, USA
"Roundtrip Beijing—New York Now Selections From The Domus Collection", Ullens Center for Contemporary Art, Beijing, China
"Negotiations—the Second Today's Documents", Pifo New Art Gallery, Beijing, China
"Trap", Art Issue Projects, Beijing, China
"Beyond Fashion--1st Crossover between Young Chinese Fashion Designers and Young Chinese Artists", Beyond Art Space, Beijing, China
"Internationale Lichttage Winterthur 2010", Winterthur, Switzerland
"Community of Tastes: Chinese Contemporary Art Since 2000", Museum of Contemporary Art Santiago, Chile

2009
"Luminal Art", Gallery 100,Taipei, Taiwan, China
Art in Busan 2009 "Inter-City", Busan Museum of Modern Art, Busan, Korea
"Grand Opening of White Box Museum of Art and The Home Court: An Exhibition of Contemporary Art", White Box Museum of Art, Beijing, China

2008
"Facing Reality", National Art Museum of China, Beijing, China
"International Exhibition of Sculptures and Installations", Venice Lido, Venice, Italy
"Turn and Widen—the 5th Seoul International Media Art Biennale Seoul Museum of Art", Seoul, Korea
"The Love of Art - Collecting Contemporary Art in China", Today Art Museum, Beijing, China

2007
"EXIT Festival", the Maison des Arts et de la Culture of Créteil (MAC), Paris, France
"VIA festival", the Manège of Maubeuge, Maubeuge, France
"MIRAGE", Oriental Vista Art Collectio, Shanghai, China
"Sensitivity", Dimensons Art Centre, Beijing, China
"2007 Beijing 798 Art Festival", Beijing Da Shan Zi 798, Beijing, China
Floating - New Generation of Art in China, National Museum of Contemporary Art, Seoul, Korea
"China: Face the reality", Museum of Moderner Kunst Stiftung Ludwig Wien,Vienna, Austria

2006
"2006 Busan Biennial", Naru Park, Busan, Korea
"Cold Energy", PYO Gallery, Beijing, China
"Made in China", Public piaces, Berlin, Germany
"2006 Shanghai Biennial", Shanghai Art Museum, Shanghai, China
"Unclear and Clearness", Heyri Asia Project I,

Seoul, Korea
"Er Ti Jiao", Beijing TangRen Contemporary Art Centre, Beijing, China
"Asia Contemporary Art", Loop Art Centre, Seoul, Korea
"Free Walk", Osage Gallery, Hong Kong, China

2005
"Transparent Box", Jian Wai SOHO, Beijing, China
"2005 Chengdu Biennial", Contemporary Art Museum, Chengdu, China
"Ten Thousands years ago", Back Modern City, Beijing, China
"Fictitious Love", Shanghai Moca Art Museum, Shanghai, China
"The Other End", He Xiangning Art Museum, Shenzhen, China

2004
"Playing with Chi Energy", House of Shiseido, Tokyo, Japan

2003
"Sculpture Exhibition", Tokyo Gallery, Beijing, China
"Driftage", Back Modern City, Beijing, China
"Consubstantiality of Male and Female", 798 Western Art Section, Beijing, China

2002
"International City Sculpture Exhibition", Beijing Sculpture Park, Beijing, China

095

[李继开]

1975 生于四川成都
2004 毕业于四川美术学院油画系获硕士学位
现任教于湖北美术学院动画学院

获奖信息
2010
第二届报喜鸟新锐艺术人物大奖
2005
未来考古学——第二届中国艺术家三年展大奖

个展
2011
“状态”，李继开个展，第三届报喜鸟新锐艺术人物盛典，鲁迅美术学院，沈阳，中国
“有，没有”，李继开个展，对画空间，北京，中国

2010
灯笼——李继开个展，美术文献艺术中心，武汉，湖北，中国
思虑，Canvas 国际艺术画廊，阿姆斯特丹，荷兰

2009
李继开，阿拉里奥画廊，首尔，韩国
留一点想象空间——李继开 \ 王劲松双个展，对画空间，北京，中国

2008
清空——李继开个展，今日美术馆，北京，中国
乱枝——李继开的绘画，美术文献艺术中心，武汉，湖北，中国
独自行走，Canvas 国际艺术画廊，阿姆斯特丹，荷兰
小世界——李继开的绘画，季节画廊，苏黎士，瑞士
暗夜时光流过——李继开 2008 作品展，美术文献艺术中心，武汉，湖北，中国
混沌，当代唐人艺术中心，香港，中国
2007 清空——李继开个展，上海美术馆，上海，中国
男孩与镜像，Christa Schuebbe 画廊，杜塞尔多夫，德国

群展
2011
台北艺术博览会，对画空间，台北，中国
城市图景，中国美术学院美术馆，杭州，浙江，中国
回顾与展望——湖北油画艺术展，武汉美术馆，武汉，湖北，中国
旧事，前进当代画廊，上海，中国
图书馆计划——个人、公共、文献展，重庆市渝中区图书馆，重庆，中国
艺术北京——2011 当代艺术博览会，对画空间，全国农业展览馆，北京，中国

2010
共鸣——中法艺术邀请展，武汉美术馆，武汉，湖北，中国
迈阿密国际艺术博览会，对画空间， 迈阿密，美国
后叙事，别处空间，北京，中国
Pan- 阿姆斯特丹艺术博览会，阿姆斯特丹，荷兰
台北艺术博览会，对画空间，台北，中国
围城，美术文献艺术中心，武汉，湖北，中国
“图像经验——2010 当代艺术邀请展”，江山美术馆，重庆，中国
现实的游牧——进入文化裂变的当代，现·实空间，798 艺术区，北京，中国
2010 中国国际画廊博览会（CIGE），对画空间，北京国贸中心，北京，中国
艺术北京，2010 当代艺术博览会，北京，中国
第 26 届阿姆斯特丹国际艺术博览会 ART AMSTERDAM，阿姆斯特丹，荷兰
滤窗——中国青年艺术家群展，别处空间，北京，中国
改造历史——2000-2009 年的中国新艺术，国家会议中心，北京，中国
Franks-Suss 收藏展，萨奇画廊，伦敦，英国

2009
真实的真实，迈阿密国际艺术博览会，迈阿密，美国
李继开 +Unmask，H.T gallery，798 艺术区，北京，中国
动漫美学双年展 2009-2010，今日美术馆，北京，中国
Art Cars，萨迪亚特，迪拜，阿联酋
与上文相关——当代绘画展，铸造艺术馆，北京，中国
同行德中，武汉美术馆，武汉，湖北，中国
之乎者也——艺术修辞学，红星画廊，798 艺术区，北京，中国
重庆双年展，重庆会展中心，重庆，中国
常态——2009 年作品展，美术文献艺术中心新空间，武汉，湖北，中国
留一点想象空间——李继开 / 王劲松双个展，对画空间，北京，中国
新浪潮，新力量——15 位中国新兴艺术家，林大画廊，雅加达，印尼
China Mania，阿肯当代美术馆，哥本哈根，丹麦
展望，奥美零空间，北京，中国
在场三十年——四川美术学院当代油画展，日中友好会馆美术馆，日本，东京
两湖潮流——湖南·湖北当代艺术展 1985—2009，广东美术馆，广东，中国
2009 中国国际画廊博览会，北京国贸中心，北京，中国
艺术北京——2009 当代艺术博览会，全国农业展览馆，北京，中国
新潮流——十五位当代中国艺术家联展，太平洋传统博物馆，旧金山，美国
动漫美学百相，印尼国家美术馆，印尼
都市中——中国当代艺术选展，子午线国际中心，华盛顿哥伦比亚特区，美国
超越全球化——泛亚洲当代艺术联展，别处空间，北京，中国
Pan- 阿姆斯特丹艺术博览会，阿姆斯特丹，荷兰
巴塞尔艺术博览会，巴塞尔，瑞士

2008
阿迪达斯：共震——运动视界艺术展，上海、广州、南京、沈阳、成都、北京，中国
迷宫，艺识空间，酒厂艺术区 F3，北京，中国
“纸上图画”，美术文献艺术中心，武汉，湖北，中国
时差：中国当代艺术新力量，玛吉画廊，马德里，西班牙
飞地：中国当代新绘画，南京四方当代美术馆，南京，江苏，中国
截点，OV 画廊，香港，中国
“重建——地震灾区捐赠展”，星空间，798 艺术区，北京，中国
“自由活动——年青艺术家项目”，美术文献艺术中心，武汉，湖北，中国
别处卡通——亚洲当代艺术联展，别处空间，798 艺术区，北京，中国
个案——艺术史和艺术批评中的艺术家，圣之空间

艺术中心，798 艺术区，北京
源：第一届月亮河雕塑艺术节，月亮河当代艺术馆，北京，中国
陈可、李继开、仇晓飞、申亮，DF2 画廊，洛杉矶，美国
萌，中国广场画廊，纽约，美国
后场，别处空间，798 艺术区，北京，中国
拓展与融合——中国现代油画研究展，中国美术馆，北京，中国
“亚洲方位——第三届南京三年展”，南京博物院，南京，江苏，中国
“梦蝶——第二届上海当代艺术馆文献展”，上海当代艺术馆，上海，中国
转世肉身，柏林，德国
“找自己”，民生艺术中心，上海，中国
Cathrine Raben Davidsen & 李继开联展，丹麦艺术中心，北京，中国
契・吸引力，中德新锐艺术家联展，OV 画廊，上海，中国
扮傻游戏：一次从规训社会的虚拟出走，天画廊，北京，中国；首尔，韩国
画中有话，对画空间，北京，中国
新中国当代，迈阿密艺术博览会，迈阿密，美国
“互动——2008 中国当代油画邀请展”，武汉美术馆，武汉，湖北，中国
Pan- 阿姆斯特丹艺术博览会，阿姆斯特丹，荷兰
动漫美学百像，印度尼西亚国家美术馆，雅加达，印尼
2008 中国国际画廊博览会，北京国贸中心，北京，中国

2007
媒介和传统的当代道路——中国当代雕塑十人展，亚洲艺术中心，北京，中国
抽离中心的一代——70 后艺术展，798 艺术区 706 厂房，北京，中国
面貌，奥美零空间，北京，中国
“没有你，没有我”，宋庄美术馆，北京，中国
1976-2006 乡土现代性到都市乌托邦——“四川画派”学术回顾展，中国美术馆，北京，中国
视觉遭遇，中国美术馆，北京，中国
纪事，美域，未来——70 后新锐艺术展，当代唐人艺术中心，曼谷，泰国
“武汉！武汉！”，四方当代美术馆，南京，江苏，中国
世事而非——真实形象的变异及探索，斗山艺术中心，首尔，韩国
2007 年首届今日文献展——能量：精神・身体・物质，今日美术馆，北京，中国
中国首次赴日当代艺术展，东京国家艺术俱乐部，日本
陈可、李继开、韦嘉，Thomas Erben 画廊，纽约，美国
亚洲制造，Opera 画廊，香港，中国
从未出现过的变化——来自中国的新艺术，季节画廊，苏黎士，瑞士
非集体意志——武汉 70 后当代艺术展，索卡艺术中心，北京，中国
西游记——中国新故事，Kunstraum Noe
Niederȯsterreichische 美术馆，维也纳，奥地利
Pan- 阿姆斯特丹艺术博览会，阿姆斯特丹，荷兰
迈阿密艺术博览会，迈阿密，美国
2007 中国国际画廊博览会，北京国贸中心，北京，中国
今日中国，COBRA 博物馆，阿姆斯特丹，荷兰
新青年，江汉大学美术馆，武汉，湖北，中国

2006
超越的维度：中国新绘画，四方当代美术馆，南京，江苏，中国
自我造局：2005 中国当代绘画展，上海证大现代艺术馆，上海，中国
日纪与绎言：当代艺术展，北城天街，龙湖，重庆，中国
新年快乐：年轻一代油画作品展，美术文献艺术中心，武汉，湖北，中国
非常印象：后生代油画作品展，今日美术馆，北京，中国
遭喻现实，重庆美术馆，重庆，中国
世界杯美丽足球 11×11 涂鸦艺术展，上海中信泰富广场，上海，中国
重庆辣椒，青岛美术馆，青岛，中国
新界面——UP 新一代登陆展，刘海粟美术馆，上海，中国
2006 年中国国际画廊博览会，北京国贸中心，北京，中国
SATELLITE2006 当代艺术暨设计年展，Vanguard 画廊，上海，中国
潜在的交流——中国—奥地利年轻艺术家的派对，南视觉美术馆，南京，江苏，中国
变异的图像——中国当代油画邀请展，上海美术馆，上海，中国
超验的中国，阿拉里奥画廊，北京，中国
李继开 + 陈波新作展，美术文献艺术中心，武汉，湖北，中国
KIAF2006 韩国国际艺术博览会，韩国
台北国际艺术博览会，台北，台湾，中国
杜塞尔多夫艺术博览会，杜塞尔多夫，德国
艺术北京 2006，当代艺术博览会，北京，中国
“机会主义的秋天”，美术文献艺术中心，武汉，湖北，中国

2005
“下一站，卡通吗？”，星空间艺术中心，北京；何香凝美术馆，深圳；重庆美术馆，重庆，中国
低和浅的游戏——漫画一代的崛起，3818 库画廊，798 艺术区，北京，中国
未来考古学——第二届中国艺术三年展，南京博物院，南京，江苏，中国
70 后艺术——市场改变中国之后的一代，明园文化艺术中心，上海；今日美术馆，北京，中国
限制与自由——夏市，美术文献艺术中心，武汉，湖北，中国
西门子艺术项目：他们在这做什么——WH.S+8，西门子武汉分公司，武汉，湖北，中国
一卡通，泰康人寿顶层空间，北京，中国
寓・言——现实深处：中国当代艺术展，六合天寓地库，杭州，中国
温暖——中国当代艺术展，红桥画廊，上海，中国
坏孩子的天空——70 后的问题青年，3818 库画廊，798 艺术区，北京，中国

2004
轻装上路——重庆 & 香港艺术交流展，艺术公社国际展览馆，香港、重庆，中国
通道——中法文艺走廊，重庆美术馆、巴黎，中国、法国
少年心气——中国新锐绘画，何香凝美术馆、中央美术学院，深圳、北京，中国
模糊摩擦——首届美术文献提名外围展，湖北省美术馆，武汉，湖北，中国
恭喜发财、鱼目混珠、狐假虎威——首届美术文献提名外围展，武汉，湖北，中国
花花世界——中国油画新新力量 2004 年展，上海、广州、北京，中国
划痕——当代中国独立影像展映（重庆站），家・M 公社，重庆，中国

2003
方向——四川美术学院“中国元素”学术主题年系列展，重庆，中国
十三人作品展，重庆，中国
形蚀——李继开 + 刘靖作品展，重庆，中国

2002
Fun 视觉展，家・M 公社，重庆，中国
实验中的美术——重庆美术馆开幕展，重庆美术馆，重庆

出版
2006
《李继开》/ 南画廊，南京
2007
《李继开》/ 上海人民美术出版社
《李继开》/ 项目，杜塞尔多夫，德国
2008
《小世界》/ 瑞士季节画廊，苏黎世
《乱枝》/ 美术文献艺术中心，武汉
《混浊》/ 当代唐人艺术中心，香港
《断木森林》/ 美术文献艺术中心，武汉
2009
《留一点想象空间》/ 中国今日美术馆出版社
《独自行走》/ 阿姆斯特丹国际油画艺术，荷兰
2010
《思虑》/ 阿姆斯特丹国际油画艺术，荷兰
《灯笼——李继开个展》/ 美术文献艺术中心，武汉
《一个人的低吟浅唱——李继开作品集》/ 文化艺术出版社，北京

[Li JiKai]

1975 Born in Chengdu, China
2004 Graduated with MFA from Sichuan Fine Arts Instiute, China

Currently works in Hubei Institute of Fine Arts

Awards

2010

The second BaoxiNiao Cutting-edge Art Aharacters Award

2005

Archeology of the Future-The Second Triennial of Chinese Artists Award

Solo Exhibitions

2011

Existential condition, The morality of Li Jikai's painting, Luxun Academy of Fine Arts, Shenyang, China

Someting,or Noting, Li Jikai Solo Exhibition, Dialogue Space, Beijing, China

2010

Lantern - Li Jikai Solo Exhibition, Fine Arts Literature Art Center, Wuhan, Hubei, China

Reflection - Canvas International Art, Amsterdam, Holland

2009

Li Jikai, Arario GallerymSeoul, Korea

Leaving Some Room For Imagination - Dual Exhibition of Li Jikai and Wang Jingsong, Dialogue Space, Beijing, China

2008

"Clear", Today Art Museum, Beijing, China

"Unorderly Branches": Paintings of Li Jikai, Fine Arts Literature Art Center, Wuhan, Hubei, China

Walking alone, Canvas International Art, Amsterdam, Holland

Small Worlds: Paintings of Li Jikai, Art Seasons, Zurich, Switzerland

Time Flows Away at Night: 2008 Li Jikai's Works Exhibition, Fine Arts Literature Art Center, Wuhan, Hubei, China

Muddy, Tang Contemporary Art, Hong Kong, China

2007

"Clear", Shanghai Museum of Fine Arts, Shanghai, China

Boy and His Mirror Image, Christa Schuebbe Gallery, Düsseldorf, Germany

Group Exhibitions

2011

Art Taipei, Dialogue Space, Taipei,China

City Picture, Art Museum of China Academy of Art, Hangzhou, Zhejiang, China

Retrospect and Prospect—Hubei Oil Painting Art Exhibition, Wuhan Art Museum, Wuhan, Hubei, China

Reminiscence, Front Line Contemporary Gallery, Shanghai, China

Library Project-Individual, blic, Documentary, Chongqing Library, Chongqing, China

Art Beijing, 2011 Contemporary Art Fair, Dialogue Space, Beijing, China

2010

Resonances, Sino-French Art Communication ExhibitionWuhan Art Museum, Wuhan, Hubei, China

Miami International Art Fair, Dialogue Space, Miami, America

Post—Narration, Beyond Art Space, Beijing, China

Pan—Amsterdam Art Fair, Amsterdam, Holland

Taipei Art Fair, DialogueSpace, Taipei, Taiwan, China

Fortress Besieged, Fine Arts Literature Art Center, Wuhan, Hubei, China

"Image Experience"2010 Contemporary Art Exhibition, Jiangshan Art Museum, Chongqing, China

Nomadic Reality -Into Contemporaneity with Fractured Culture, Esse Art Space, 798 Art zone, Beijing, China

CIGE2010(China International Gallery Exposition 2010), Dialogue Space Gallery, China World Trade Center, Beijing, China

Art Beijing, 2010 Contemporary Art Fair, Beijing, China

26th International Art Fair in Amsterdam(ART AMSTERDAM), Amsterdam, Holland

Filter Window -Young Chinese Artists Group Exhibition, Beyond Art Space, Beijing, China

Reshaping History, Chinart from 2000 to 2009, China National Convention Center, Beijing, China

The Franks-Suss Collection, Saatchi Gallery, London, United Kingdom

2009

Truly Truthful, Art Asia Miami, USA

Lijikai+Unmask, H.T Gallery, 798 Art Area, Beijing, China

Animamix Biennial 2009 - 2010, Today Art Museum, Beijing, China

Related to the context - Contemporary Painting Exhibition, Found Museum, Beijing, China

Art Cars, Saadiyat island, Abu Dhabi, The United Arab Emirates

Chongqing Biennale, Chongqing Exhibition Center, Chongqing, China

Gemeinsam in Bewegung - Zeitgenössische Kunst aus Deutschland und China, Wuhan Art Museum, Wuhan, Hubei, China

Normality - 2009 Art Works Show, New Space of Fine Arts Literature Art Center, Wuhan, Hubei, China

Leaving Some Room For Imagination - Dual Exhibition of Li Jikai and Wang Jingsong, Dialogue Space Gallery, Beijing, China

New Wave, New Power-15 Young Emerging Artists From China, Malinda Art Gallery, Jakarta, Indonesia

China Mania, Arken Art Museum, Copenhagen, Denmark

Revealing Expectations, Ogilvy O Gallery, Beijing, China

Sichuan School- Sichuan Fine Arts Institute in Japan Exhibition, Japan-China

Friendship Center Gallery, Tokyo, Japan

Hunan and Hubei Trend- Hunan, Hubei Exhibition of Contemporary Art 1985-200, Guangdong Museum of Art, Guangdong, China

CIGE 2009 (China International Gallery Exposition 2009), China World Trade Center, Beijing, China

Art Beijing 09, Art Beijing Contemporary Art Fair, Agricultural Exhibition Center, Beijing, China

New Trends: Fifteen Contemporary Chinese Artists, The Pacific Heritage Museum, San Francisco, USA

100 tales in Animamix, Indonesia National Art Museum, Indonesia

Metropolis Now - A Selection of Chinese of Contemporary Art, Meridian Center, Washington, USA

Beyond Globalization - Pan-Asia Contemporary Art Group Exhibition, Beyond Art Space, Beijing, China

ART AMSTERDAM Art Fair, Amsterdam, Netherlands

Art Basel, Basel, Switzerland

2008

Adidas: A Total Shock - Sports'Horizon Art Exhibition, Shanghai, Guangzhou, Nanjing, Shenyang, Chengdu, Beijing, China

Labyrinth, Art and Knowledge Space, F3, Brewery Art Complex, Beijing, China

"Works on Paper", The Center for Art Archives, Wuhan, Hubei, China

Time Difference: the New Force in Chinese Contemporary Art, Magee Art Gallery, Madrid, Spain

The Soaring Field: New Paintings from China, Nanjing Square Art Museum, Nanjing, Jiangsu, China

Cross-Section, Oriental Vista Gallery, Hong Kong, China

"Reconstruct" - Donating Exhibition for Earthquake-stricken-area, Star Gallery, Beijing 798, Beijing, China

"Free exercise" Young Artist Projects, The Center for Art Archives, Wuhan, Hubei, China

Beyond Cartoon - Asian Contemporary Art Group, Beyond Art Space, Beijing 798, Beijing, China
Case Studies of Artists in Art History and Art Criticism, SZ Art Center, 798 Art Area, Beijing, China
The Origin: The First Annual Moon River Sculpture Festival, MR MOCA (The Moon River Museum of Contemporary Art), Beijing, China
Chenke, Lijikai, Chouxiaofei, Shenliang, DF2 Gallery, Los Angeles, America
Germinators, China Square Gallery, New York, USA
Waiting in the Wings, beyond art space, 798 Art Area, Beijing, China
Expand & Fusion-Chinese Oil Painting Study And Exhibition, National Art Museum Of China, Beijing, China
"Reflective Asia" - 3rd Nanjing Triennial, Nanjing, Jiangsu, China
"Butterfly Dream" - Shanghai MOCA Envisage II, MOCA Shanghai, Shangha, China
Transgressive Body, Berlin, Germany
Looking for me, Minsheng Art Museum Update, Shanghai, China
Cathrine Raben Davidsen & Li Jika, dARTex(The Danish Art Exchange), Beijing, China
Contracts-Affinity, Oriental Vista Gallery, Shanghai, China
Game of acting the fool, Gallery TN, Beijing, China and Seoul, Korea
Conversation in Paintings, Dialogue Space Gallery, Beijing, China
New China Contemporary, ABMB(Art Basel-Miami Beach), Miami, USA
"Interaction" - New 2008 Invitational Exhibition of Contemporary Chinese Oil Paintings, Wuhan Art Museum, Wuhan, Hubei, China
Pan-Amsterdam Art Fair, Amsterdam, Netherlands
100 Tales in Anima mix, Indonesia national gallery, Jakarta, Indonesia
CIGE2008(China International Gallery Exposition 2008), China World Trade Center, Beijing, China

2007

The Contemporary Way of Media and Tradition - Ten Contemporary Chinese Sculptors, Asian Art Center, Beijing, China
The Generation without a Center - The Art of post 70's, 706 Factory, 798Art Area, Beijing, China
Outlook, Ogilvy O Gallery, Beijing, China
Without You, Without Me, Songzhuang Art Museum, Beijing, China
From Rural Modernity to Urban Utopia - A Retrospective of Sichuan School of Painting, 1976-2006, National Art Museum of China, Beijing, China
Visual Experiences, National Art Museum of China, Beijing, China
Narrative, Fantasy, Future - Exhibition of post 70's New Art, Tang Contemporary Art Gallery, Bangkok, Thailand
Wuhan! Wuhan! Nanjing Square Contemporary Art Museum, Nanjing, Jiangsu, China
Things Do Not - Variations and Explorations of True Images, Doosan Art Center, Seoul, Korea
The first today's Documents 2007 - Energy: Spiril, Boday, Material, Today Art Museum, Beijing, hina
China's First Contemporary Art Exposition in Japan, Tokyo National Arts Club, Japan
Chen Ke, Li Jikai, Wei Jia, Thomas Erben Gallery, New York, USA
Made in Asia, Opera Gallery, Hong Kong, China
There Has Never Been A Change - New Art From China, Art Seasons, Zurich, Switzerland
Uncollectivism - Exhibition of Wuhan's Post 70's Arts, Suoka Arts Centre, Beijing, China
The Journey to the West - A Chinese New Story, Kunstraum Noe Niederösterreichische Museum, Vienna, Austria
Pan-Amsterdam Art Fair, Amsterdam, the Netherlands
Art Basel Miami, Miami, USA
CIGE 2007(China International Gallery Exposition 2007), China World Trade Center, Beijing, China
China Now Now! Cobra Museum, Amsterdam, the Netherlands
New Youth, Jianghan University Gallery, Wuhan, Hubei, China

2006

Beyond Dimension: Chinese New Painting, Nanjing Square Contemporary Art Museum, Nanjing, Jiangsu, China
The Self - Made Situation: A Retrospective of New Chinese Painting 2005, Shanghai Zendai Museum of Modern Art, Shanghai, China
Blog and Statement: Contemporary Art Exhibition, Beicheng Tianjie, Longhu, Chongqing, China
Happy New Year: Oil Painting by Young Artists, Art Archive Art Centre, Wuhan, Hubei, China
Unusual Impression: Oil Painting by post-Cenozoic, Today Art Museum, Beijing, China
Reality in Metaphor, Congqing Art Museum, Chongqing, China
World Cup Beautiful Football 11x11 Doodle Exhibition, CITIC Plaza, Shanghai, China
Chongqing Chili, Qingdao Art Museum, Qingdao, China
New Interface-Debut of UP Generation, Liu Haisu Art Museum, Shanghai, China
CIGE2006(China International Gallery Exposition 2006), China World Trade Center, Beijing, China
SATELLITE 2006 Contemporary Art & Design Exhibition, Vanguard Gallery, Shanghai, China
Potential Dialogue - The party of Sino-Austria young artists, Nanjing RCM Museum, Nanjing, Jiangsu, China
Varied Images-Invitation Exhibition of chiniese Contemporary Paintings, Sanghai Art Museum, Shanghai, China
Beyond Experience: New China! Arario Gallery, Beijing, China
New works by Chen Bo and Li Jikai, Fine Arts Literature Art Center, Wuhan
KIAF 2006 Korea International Art Fair, Seoul, Korea
Art Taipei, Taipei, Taiwan, China
Art Fair Dusseldorf, Dusseldorf, Germany
Art Beijng 2006, Art Beijng Contemporary Art Fair, Beijing, China
The Autumn for Opportunists, Fine Arts Literature Art Center, Wuhan, Hubei, China

2005

Next Station, Cartoon? Star Gallery, He xiangning Art Museum, Chongqing Art Museum, Beijing, Shenzhen, Chongqing, China
A Low and Shallow Game: the Rise of the Cartoon Generation, 3818 Cool Gallery, Beijing 798, Beijing, China
Future Archeology: The Second Triennial Exhibition of Chinese Art, Nanjing Museum, Nanjing, Jiangsu, China
After 1970s: The Generation Changed by Market, Mingyuan Art Center, Today Art Museum, Shanghai, Beijing, China
Limitation and Freedom - Summer, Fine Arts Literature Art Center, Wuhan, Hubei, China
Siemens Arts Program: What are They Doing Here? - WH.S+8, Siemens, Wuhan, Hubei, China
Multi-Purpose Card, The Top Floor Space of Taikang Life Insurance Company Ltd, Beijing, China
Metaphor-Language-In the Depth of Reality: Chinese Contemporary Art Exhibition, Basement of Liuhe Apartment, Hangzhou, China
Warm: Chinese Contemporary Art Exhibition, Red Bridge Gallery, Shanghai, China
The Sky of Bad Children - Delinquent Juvenile Born in the 1970s, 3818 Cool Gallery, Beijing 798, Beijing, China

2004

Light Load to Start - Exchange Exhibition between Chongqing and Hong Kong, Hong Kong Art Commune, Hong Kong, Chongqing, China
Passage - Sino-French Art Gallery, Chongqing Art Museum, Paris, China, France
Young Spirit - New Chinese Painting, He xiangning Art Museum, Central Academy of Fine Arts, Shenzhen, Beijing, China
Fuzzy Friction - The First Art Document Nomination Exhibition, Hubei Art Museum, Wuhan, Hubei, China
Congratulations for Getting Rich, Sell Fish Eyes for Pearls and Ass in the Lion's Skin - The First Art Document Nomination Exhibition, Wuhan, Hubei, China
Colorful World-Exhibition of New Chinese Painting Genre in 2004, Shanghai, Guangzhou and Beijing, China
Scarify - China Modern Independent Image Exhibition, Home·M Commune, Chongqing, China

2003
Direction - the Series Exhibition of Chinese Elements Academic Year of Sichuan Fine Arts Institute, Chongqing, China
Exhibition of Thirteen Persons' Works, Chongqing, China
Shape Erosion - Exhibition of Li Jikai and Liu Jing's Works, Chongqing, China

2002
Fun Visual Exhibition, Home·M Commune, Chongqing, China
Art in Experimentation:An Exhibition for the Inauguration of Chongqing Art Museum, Chongqing Art Museum, Chongqing, China

Publishing
2006
《LI Jikai NOTE》/ RCM Gallery
2007
《LI JiKai》/ Shanghai People's Art Press
《Li Jikai》/ SCHUEBBE PROJECTS, Dǔsseldorf, Germany
2008
《SMALL WORLDS》 Switzerland Seasons Gallery, Zurich
《Arbitrary Branch》/ Arts and Literature Center, Wuhan
《Turbid》/ Tang Contemporary Art Center, Hong Kong
《Broken Wood Forest》/ Arts and Literature Center, Wuhan
2009
《Leaving some room for imagination》/ China Today Art Museum Publishing House
《WALKNING ALONE-PAINTINGS BY LI JIKAI》/ Amsterdam Canvas International Art, Netherlands
2010
《REFLECTIONS-PAINTINGS BY LI JIKAI》/ Amsterdam Canvas International Art, Netherlands
《Lantern-Li Jikai Solo Exhibition》/ Arts and Literature Center, Wuhan
《The Solitary Musings of a Silent Soul-A collection of Li Jikai's works》/ Culture and Art Publishing House, Beijing

113

[屠宏涛]

1976 生于四川成都
1998 获台湾李仲生基金会优秀奖
1999 毕业于中国美院油画系

个展
2011
当代"植物的欲望——屠宏涛新作展"，伊比利亚艺术中心，北京，中国

2008
"幻觉乐园"，玛吉画廊，马德里，西班牙
"迷局"，中国当代画廊，纽约，美国

2007
"交织"，索卡当代空间，北京，中国
"探索"，Olivia Oriental 画廊，伦敦，英国

群展
2011
"引领风骚"，索卡十年，北京，中国
"趣味的共同——2000年以来的中国当代艺术"，巴西
《大周末 Hotspot》四周年庆典暨首届"城市趣味"明星名人当代艺术推荐收藏展，北京，中国
"飞越对流层——新一代绘画备忘录"，伊比利亚当代艺术中心，北京，中国
"溪山清远"，亚洲美术馆，旧金山，美国
"中国式书写"，今日美术馆，北京，中国
"欲 —— 病理与凝视"，A4画廊，成都，中国
"无法缺席"，文轩美术馆，成都，中国

2010
"改造历史"，中国国际会议中心，北京，中国
"滤窗"，别处空间画廊，北京，中国
"可见的部分"，廊桥艺术中心，成都，中国

2009
"布拉格双年展 —— 中国盒子"，布拉格，捷克
"方言的性格"，蓝顶美术馆，成都，中国
"反光：新艺术的纵深"，西湖美术馆，杭州；墙美术馆，北京，中国
"工作坊"，伊比利亚当代艺术中心，北京，中国
"失乐园"，方音画廊，北京，中国

2008
"自然的消失"，艺术方位画廊，深圳，中国
"数像时代的绘画与雕塑"，空港十号，成都，中国
"生命的状态 —— 中国东·西"，南京凤凰出版社，中国
"欲像之二"，苏州美术馆，苏州，中国
"KIAF 韩国国际艺术博览会"，首尔 COEX 中心，首尔，韩国
"成都与青岛当代艺术对话"，青岛天元美术馆，青岛，中国
"双城计"，青和当代美术馆，南京，中国
"风景的拓扑"，玛吉画廊，北京，中国
"时差：中国当代艺术新力量"，玛吉画廊，马德里，西班牙

2007
"蓝顶三年"，蓝顶艺术中心，成都，中国
"从西南出发"，广州美术馆，广州，中国
"何去何从"，香港大学博物馆，香港，中国
"贵州双年展"，贵阳市美术馆，贵阳，中国
"ART BEIJING 艺术北京博览会"，北京农展馆，北京，中国
"上海艺术博览会国际当代艺术展"，上海展览中心，上海，中国
"欲象"，宋庄美术馆，北京，中国
"动漫美学双年展"，上海当代美术馆，上海，中国

2006
"虚拟的爱"，上海当代艺术馆，上海，中国
"ARCO 艺术博览会"，西班牙
"CIGE 北京国际艺术博览会"，北京国际展览中心，北京，中国
"三台山的日子"，玉兰堂画廊，北京，中国
"虚虚实实"，韩国 HEYRI 艺术基金会，韩国
"超越维度 —— 当代艺术展"，南京四方美术馆，南京，中国
"变异的图像 —— 中国当代油画邀请展"，上海美术馆，上海，中国
"连城诀：新都市中的视觉创造"，上海证大现代艺术馆，上海，中国

2005
居住在成都 —— 油画展"，成都现代美术馆，成都，中国
"18人 —— 当代艺术展"，斯民艺苑，新加坡
"北京的天空下"，怡景苑画廊，北京，中国
"十点十色"，索卡当代空间，北京，中国

2004
"并轨，错轨 —— 当代艺术展"，成都东站艺术工作室，成都，中国
"居住在成都 —— 深圳当代油画展"，深圳美术馆，

深圳，中国
“上下左右”，成都现代美术馆，成都，中国

[Tu Hongtao]

Born 1976 in Chengdu , Sichuan China. In 1988 he received the Scholarship of Taiwan Li Zhongsheng Foundation. In 1999 he graduated from the China Academy of Fine Arts with a B.F.A. degree in Oil Painting.

Solo Exhibitions

2011
Desire of Plants - Solo Exhibition of New Oils, Iberia Center for Contemporary Art, Beijing, China

2008
Phantasmic Paradise, Magee Art Gallery Madrid, Spain
Labyrinth, Chinese Contemporary Gallery, New York, U.S.A.

2007
Interlaçe, Soka Contemporary Space, Beijing, China
Explore, Olyvia Oriental Gallery, London, U.K.

Selected Group Exhibitions

2011
Commemoration -10th Anniversary of Soka Art, Beijing, China
Comunidad De Gustos Community of Tastes - Chinese Contemporary Art Since 2000 MAC, MAC USP, Chile and Brazil
Flying through the Troposphere: Memo of New Generation Painting, Iberia Center for Contemporary Art, Beijing, China
Pure Views: New Painting from China Asian Art Museum of San Francisco, U.S.A
Chinese Painting Style,Today Art Museum, Beijing, China
Desire - Pathology and Gaze, A4 Contemporary Arts Center, Chengdu, China
Don't be absent, Chengdu Wenxuan Art Museum, Chengdu, China

2010
Reshaping History - Chinese art from 2000 to 2009 China National Convention Center, Beijing, China
Filter Window - Young Chinese Artists Group Exhibition, Beyond Art Space, Beijing, China
Visible Parts, Re-c Art Spac, Chengdu, China

2009
The 4th Prague Biennial: China Box, Prague, The Czech Republic
Character of the Dialect, Blue Roof Art Museum, Chengdu, China
Reflection, West Lake Museum of Fine Arts, The Wall Museum, China
Workshop Iberia Center for Contemporary Art Beijing, China
Lost Paradise, FFINE Gallery, Beijing, China

2008
Natural Disappearance J&Z Gallery, Shenzhen, China
Painting and Sculpture in Digital Times No. 10 Gallery of Art, Chengdu, China
Status of Life - East and West of China Phoenix Publishing House, China
Images Of Desire No.2, Suzhou Museum Suzhou, China
Korea International Art Fair, COEX, Seoul, Korea
Dialogue of Contemporary Art between Chengdu & Qingdao, Qingdao Tianyuan Art Museum, China
A Tale of Two Cities, Qinghe Contemporary Art Museum, Nanjing, China
Landscape Topology, Magee Art Gallery (Beijing), China
Time Lag -The New Force of Chinese Contemporary Art, Magee Art Gallery, Madrid, Spain

2007
Three Years in Blue House, Blue House Art Center, Chengdu, China
Starting From Southwest, Guangdong Art Museum, Guangzhou, China
Whither, The University Museum and Art Gallery, the University of Hong Kong, Hong Kong, China
Guizhou Biennial, Guiyang Art Museum, Guiyang, China
Art Beijing- Contemporary Art Fair, National Agriculture Exhibition Center, Beijing, China
Shanghai Contemporary Art Fair, Shanghai, China
Images of Desire, Songzhuang Art Museum, Beijing, China
Animamix: From Modernity to Eternity, The Museum of Contemporary Art, Shanghai, China

2006
Fiction @ Love, Contemporary Art Museum of Shanghai, Shanghai, China
ARCO Art Fair, Spain
China International Gallery Exposition,Beijing, China
My days at Santai Mount, Line Gallery,Beijing, China
Unclear and Clear, Heyri Art Foundation,Seoul, Korea
Overstep of Degree-Chinese New Painting, Nanjing Square Gallery of Contemporary Art, Nanjing, China
Aberrant Image -Invitational Exhibition of Contemporary Chinese Oil Paintings, Shanghai Museum Shanghai, China
Lian Cheng Jue -Visual Creativity in Urban City, Shanghai ZenDai Museum of Modern Art, Shanghai, China

2005
Living in Chengdu - Exhibition of Contemporary Oil Paintings, Chengdu Modern Art Museum Chengdu, China
18 Artists - Contemporary Art Exhibition, Soobin Art Gallery, Singapore
Under the Sky of Beijing, Yi Jing Yuan Gallery, Beijing, China
Ten Eras Ten Colors, Soka Contemporary Art Space, Beijing, China

2004
Binggui, Cuogui, Contemporary Art Exhibition, East Railway Station Studio,Chengdu,China
Living in Chengdu & Shenzhen - Contemporary Oil Painting Art Exhibition, Shenzhen Art Museum, Shenzhen, China

2001
Up-Down-Left-Right, Chengdu Modern Art Museum, Chengdu, China

129

[康海涛]

1976 生于重庆
2000 毕业于四川美术学院油画系
现居成都

个展

2009
“向内，凝视——康海涛个展”，偏锋新艺术空间，北京，中国

2001
“向内”个人画展，绵阳，四川，中国

群展

2011
新定义——70后艺术中质疑与理性，今日美术馆，北京，中国
“再现写实——架上绘画展”成都双年展2011，成都现代艺术馆，成都，中国
江汉繁星计划——70后艺术家研究展，湖北美术馆

湖北，中国
城市趣味——大闲末四周年庆典，今日美术馆，中国
他者之维——中国艺术家眼中的意大利，意大利、中国巡展，中国

2010
发现 1——中国当代新锐艺术家作品展，宋庄劲草空间，北京，中国
图像经验——2010当代艺术邀请展，重庆江山美术馆，重庆，中国
楼上的青年——2010青年批评家提名展，时代美术馆，北京，中国
艺术是什么——2010年度艺术家邀请展，时代美术馆，北京，中国
改造历史——2000-2009年的中国新艺术，国家会议中心，北京，中国
A+A第五回展，偏锋新艺术空间，北京，中国
中国当代艺术三十年，民生现代美术馆，上海，中国

2009
开放的视域——中国当代艺术展，捷克国家美术馆，捷克
时间的能量，昌阿特画廊，北京，中国

2008
"人民·历史——20世纪中国美术研究展"，中央美术学院美术馆，北京，中国
未来天空——中国当代青年艺术家提名展，今日美术馆，北京，中国
"看不见的青春——中国新锐艺术家展"，WATERGATE画廊，首尔，韩国
A+A第三回展，偏锋新艺术空间，北京，中国
A+A第三回展，上海多伦现代美术馆，上海，中国

2007
"自在方式"，偏锋新艺术空间，北京，中国
"缘自缘起"八人画展，绵阳，中国
"实人"中国当代艺术展，Southwest，得克萨斯州，美国
"进"当代艺术展，首都师范大学美术馆，北京，中国
A+A第二回展，798案 艺术实验室，北京，中国
A+A第二回展，中央美术学院陈列馆，北京，中国
A+A第二回展，四川大学美术馆，成都，中国
A+A第二回展，重庆美术馆，重庆，中国

2006
"自在方式"，偏锋新艺术空间，北京，中国
"大于北京"，今日美术馆，北京，中国
"出格"，偏锋新艺术空间，北京，中国

2005
"缘自缘起"，八人画展，绵阳，中国

2004
上海春季艺术沙龙展，上海，中国

[Kang Haitao]

1976 Born in Chongqing
2000 Graduated from Sichuan Fine Arts Academy, Oil Painting Department
Now Living in Chengdu

Solo Exhibitions

2009
"Introversion and Meditation—Solo Exhibition of Kang Haitao", PIFO New Art Gallery, Beijing, China

2001
"Inward", Solo Exhibition, Mianyang, China

Group Exhibitions

2011
Redefinition—Skepticism of Post-70s's Art, Today Art Museum, Beijing, China
"Representation of Realistic Art: Exhibition of Painting" — Chengdu Biennale 2011, Chengdu Contemporary Art Museum, Chengdu, China
"Aspects of the Other—Italy in the Eyes of Chinese Artists", Italy-China Tour Exhibition
City Gusto—The 4th Anniversary of HotSpot, Today Art Museum, Beijing, China
"From Scenery to Scenery of Culture—Post-70s Artists Research·Jianghan Stars Plan", Wuhan Art Museum, Hubei, China

2010
"New Face 1—Group Exhibition of Chinese Contemporary Art", Chintsao Space, Beijing, China
"Youth at Upstairs", Nomination Exhibition of Young Critics 2010, Times Art Museum, Beijing, China
Art Beijing 2010, National Agriculture Exhibition Center, Beijing, China
"Reshaping History—Chinart from 2000 to 2009", China National Convention Center, Beijing, China
"The Fifth A+A", PIFO New Art Gallery, Beijing, China
"Thirty Years of Chinese Contemporary Art", Minsheng Art Museum, Shanghai, China
"What is Art?", Times Art Museum, Beijing, China

2009
"Opening Vision", China Contemporary Art Exhibition,The Czech National Gallery, Prague, Czech Republic
"Time Power", Chang Art, Beijing, China

2008
"People · History - Exhibition of Studies of Chinese Art of the 20th Century", Central Academy of Fine Arts Museum, Beijing, China
"Future Sky—Chinese Contemporary Young Artists Nominated Exhibition", Today Art Museum, Beijing, China
"Invisible Youth—Young Artists Exhibition of China", Water Gate Gallery, Seoul, Korea
"A+A'2008 – The Third A+A", PIFO New Art Gallery, Beijing, China
"A+A'2008 – The Third A+A", Shanghai Duolun Museum of Modern Art, Shanghai, China

2007
"Comfortable Way", PIFO New Art Gallery, Beijing, China
"The Cause", Painting Exhibition of Eight Artists, Mianyang, China
"Substantial Man", Southwest Texas, USA
"Jin", Contemporary Art Exhibition, Capital Normal University of Fine Arts, Beijing, China
"A+A'2007 – The Second A+A", And Art Lab, Beijing, China
"A+A'2007 – The Second A+A", Gallery of Central Academy of Fine Arts, Beijing, China
"A+A'2007 – The Second A+A", Sichuan University Art Museum, Chengdu, China
"A+A'2007 – The Second A+A", Chongqing Art Museum, Chongqing, China

2006
"Comfortable Way", PIFO New Art Gallery, Beijing, China
"Greater than Beijing", Today International Gallery, Beijing, China
"Transgression", PIFO New Art Gallery, Beijing, China

2005
"The Cause", Painting Exhibition of Eight Artists, Mianyang, China

2004
Shanghai Spring Art Saloon, Shanghai, China

2001
"Special Happiness", Exhibition of Easel Paintings, Chengdu, China

147

[管　勇]

1975　生于山东菏泽
2003　毕业于天津美术学院油画系　获硕士学位
1998　毕业于天津美术学院油画系　获学士学位
现居北京

个展

多面审思·谁的新时代，新时代画廊，北京，中国
谁的新时代，多伦现代美术馆，上海，中国
幽默与经典，秦昊画廊，北京，中国

群展

2011

台北国际艺术博览会，台湾，中国
灿烂的伦理学，In·ter alia·Art Company，首尔，韩国
“过去，现在，未来——新时代 20 年回顾”，新时代画廊，台湾，中国

2010

东西论剑：美国美术馆巡展第二站，杰克逊威尔当代美术馆，佛罗里达，美国
台北国际艺术博览会，台湾，中国
楼上的青年：2010 青年批评家提名展，时代美术馆，北京，中国
“艺术是什么？”《大周末 Hotspot》3 周年庆暨 2010 年度艺术家邀请展，时代美术馆，北京，中国
中国国际画廊博览会，北京，中国

2009

台北国际艺术博览会，台湾，中国
ART Hongkong2009，香港，中国
中国国际画廊博览会，北京，中国

2008

新加坡国际艺术博览会，新加坡
未来天空：中国当代青年艺术家提名展，今日美术馆，北京，中国
“契——中德艺术家联展”，OV 画廊，上海，中国
台北国际艺术博览会，台北世界贸易中心，台湾，中国
和而不同：两岸艺术灵魂的相容，亚洲艺术中心，台湾，中国
管勇·杨起，Felix Ringel Gallery，杜塞尔多夫，德国
“Cross-section——2008 中国当代艺术展”，Kee Club，香港，中国
香港国际艺术展 (ART HK 08)，香港会议展览中心，香港，中国
创新世代·各执己见，新时代画廊，北京，中国
创新世代·各执己见，中国国际画廊博览会，北京，中国

2007

新时代·异宣言，中国国际画廊博览会，北京，中国
多元世代·固执己见，新时代画廊，北京、台湾，中国
抽离中心的一代——70 后艺术展，798 艺术区 706 厂空间，北京，中国

2006

超验的中国，阿拉里奥画廊，北京，中国
自我造局：2005 中国当代绘画展，证大美术馆，上海，中国

2005

70 后艺术，今日美术馆，北京，中国
70 后艺术，明园艺术中心，上海，中国

2004

亚洲青年艺术展，Sungsan Art-hall，釜山，韩国
中国新锐绘画展，何香凝美术馆，深圳，中国

2002

第二届平遥国际摄影年展，平遥，山西，中国
“与你有关”影像装置展，文化实验空间，天津，中国

[Guan Yong]

1975 Born in Heze, Shandong
2003 Graduated from the Oil Painting Department of Tianjin Academy of Fine Arts, MFA.
1998 Graduated from the Oil Painting Department of Tianjin Academy of Fine Arts, BFA.
Currently lives and works in Beijing

Solo Exhibitions

Multiaspect Reflection·Whose New Age, New Age Gallery, Beijing, China
Whose New Age, Duolun Museum of Modern Art, Shanghai, China
Humor and Classic, Qin Gallery, Beijing, China

Selected Group Exhibitions

2011

ART Taipei 2011, Taiwan, China
Splendid Ethics, In·ter alia·Art Company, Seoul, South Korea
"Past, Present, Future": Twenty-year Review of New Age Gallery, Taiwan, China

2010

East \West: Visually Speaking, MOCA Jackson, Florida, USA.
ART Taipei 2010, Taiwan, China
Youth at Upstairs: Nomination Exhibition by Young Critics 2010, Times Art Museum, Beijing, China
"What is Art", Times Art Museum, Beijing, China
China International Gallery Exposition(CIGE), Beijing, China

2009

ART Taipei 2009, Taiwan, China
ART Hong Kong 2009, Hong Kong, China
China International Gallery Exposition(CIGE), Beijing, China

2008

Art Singapore 2008-The Contemporary Asian Art Fair, Suntec, Singapore
Future Sky: Chinese Contemporary Young Artists Works Selection Exhibition, National Art Museum of China, Beijing, China
"Affinity" China & Germany Artists' Group Show, OV Gallery, Shanghai, China
Art Taipei 2008-Taipei International Art Fair, Taipei World Trade Center, Taiwan, China
Harmony in Diversity: Compatibility of Cross-strait Art Spirits, Asia Art Center, Taiwan, China
Guan Yong-Qi Yang, Felix Ringel Gallery, Dusseldorf, Germany
Cross-section: 2008 Chinese Contemporary Art, Kee Club, Hong Kong, China
Hong Kong International Art Exhibition, Hong Kong International Meeting Center, Hong Kong, China
The Age of Innovation·Being persistent, New Age Gallery, Beijing, China
The Age of Innovation·Being persistent, China International Gallery Exposition, Beijing, China

2007

New Age·Different Manifesto, China International Gallery Exposition, Beijing, China
The Age of Pluralism·Being Persistent, New Age Gallery, Beijing; Taiwan, China
Off-centering—the post-seventies Group Show, 706 Space, 798 International Art District, Beijing, China

2006

Beyond Experience: New China! Arario Gallery, Beijing, China
The Self-Made Generation: A Retrospective of New Chinese Contemporary, Zendai Museum of Modern Art, Shanghai, China.

2005

The post-seventies, Today Art Museum, Beijing, China
The post-seventies, Mingyuan Art Center, Shanghai, China

2004

Asian Art Exhibition, Sungsan Art-hall, Busan, Korea
Ideal of new generation: Chinese new generation artist award exhibition, He Xiangning Art Museum, Shenzhen, China.

2002

The Second Pingyao International Photography Festival, Pingyao, Shanxi, China
Have to do with you—Video and Installation exhibition, Culture Space, Tianjin, China

后 记
Afterword

从“迷失”到“理性”

——“70后”艺术中的质疑精神

杭春晓

“70后”艺术作为一个概念，主要产生于2000年以后，是对中国70年代出生的艺术家创作的群体性定位。其学术解读，多归于“卡通”、“青春残酷”两种理论体系，已形成一定的社会接受度。但现有理论阐释，要么流于简单的图像符号特征，如“卡通”之说；要么以“浅层伤害”为基点解读的青春期冲动，如“青春残酷”之说。前者，以形式符号为理论阐释，难以准确把握这一代艺术的精神诉求；而后者则建立在“70后”与其前辈的生活经历对比，因缺少各类运动的社会性深刻，所以阐释其为缺乏相应深度的“冲动”性自我感悟。此说貌似合理，但却假定了人的深刻性一定源于社会活动，而非人自身的精神审视能力，从而流于简单、臆测，无法触及这一代艺术真正的意义、价值。

那么，面对丰富复杂的70后创作，我们又该如何审视？由于，“70后”是一个时间概念，故其理论建设也应基于时代性，即线索是某一时间段中的文化问题，以及这种问题在创作中的视觉显现。所以，就“70后”艺术的理论构建而言，方法论上必然会倾向于社会学阐释，需要寻找这一时间段内社会问题在文化上的呈现与表达。然而，因为曾经流行的庸俗社会学，近年来美术界对社会学的运用多有谨慎，甚至一味排斥。当然，警惕庸俗社会学简单、机械的“社会图谱化”，对于美术理论反思具有积极意义。但，因此而完全漠视艺术与特定时间段内社会的关联，无疑又走向了另一个极端。所以，就“70后”艺术而言，我们仍然不能回避社会学的阐释方式，而是应该在充分理解他们的视觉体验之后,探寻其背后的心理发生机制。

如果，依着这一思路进行下去，“70后”艺术在视觉体验上有着怎样特征呢？应该说，相对前一代图像化平涂、矛盾化对立的视觉特征，“70后”的作品，往往更强调语言本体在视觉上的自身表达，也即习惯于视觉物质自身所具有的表达。诸如尹朝阳的“神话”、屠宏涛的“舞台”、康海涛的“夜景”等，无论表述的目标是个体化感悟，还是社会化体验，语言的物质性成为了绘画意图的直接媒介，甚至语言运用的方法成为重建视觉逻辑的核心，而非图像符号。而王光乐从超级写实的水磨石到寿漆，抽象对于艺术家而言并非一种结构的预设，而是对于视觉呈现方式的不断审视而自发的结果。又如管勇的“书架”、李晖的“双头卡车”、王颉的“无人衣”等，虽具有某种明确的题材对象，但其视觉指向却非题材本身，而是视觉逻辑自身所包含的某种认知方式与观念。并且，这种对于语言本体、视觉逻辑的重视，其背后往往蕴含了某种“不置可否”的怀疑性态度，即不对自己所描绘对象以某种肯定性或否定性的判断，而是将对象理解为借助视觉语言呈现出的认知物，并在自己的视觉逻辑中成为观者可以重新审视的对象。从某种角度上看，他们的艺术不同于“政治波普”影响下的具有某种“明确意图”的图像，他们不喜欢“口号化”的符号观念，而更愿意将视觉进行审视的行为本身展现出来。于是，即便是借助“卡通符号”的艺术家，如李继开，其画面中的卡通形象也并非某种确定性观念的符号，而是一种“不置可否”，带有迷失感的视觉情绪。应该说，这种视觉上的不确定性、迷失感，形成的一种对待事物的“质疑”姿态，于“70后”艺术中较为普遍，并明显与此前的艺术创作拉开一种距离。

所谓“质疑”姿态，就是不再简单肯定、简单否定，并对某种具体、明确的判断保持警惕。作为同年代出生的人，我对此感同身受。因为这一代人的生存体验，往往处于一种“前后矛盾”之中。众所周知，他们的成长背景，可以概括为“后理想主义”——新中国成立初期的社会理想由于文革而破灭，继而，80年代的文化理想也因90年代商业化而走向幻灭，整个社会趋于现实性的务实主义。成长于这一巨变期的“70后”一代，在人生命运上往往只有参与权，而无选择权，处于一种被动性转换与适应的过程，也即不断被迫调整、改变自己原有世界观以适应新的生活状态。在他们身上，缺乏一以贯之的社会环境与认知世界的方式，在不断自我调整的过程中形成了他们对历史、对现状的质疑；并且，这种情绪性的时代特征在他们不断自我颠覆、自我构建的过程中，形成了别具特征的精神质地——不会轻易认可，习惯以带有“迷失感”的语言质疑一切，并在这一过程中完成理性反思。

如果说，20世纪的中国一直处于一种文化嫁接的过程中，习惯从物质层面到精神层面学习西方，那么这种方式到“70后”发生了某种微妙的变化。这一代人因为个人生存际遇的特殊，导致了他们天然具有的怀疑姿态，使得他们不再迷信他者，不再简单接受任何一种非我的思想，从而也就使得中国获得了一种文化上自我审视、自我选择与自我构建的机会。虽然，这一过程仍然处于一个非结论性的发展阶段，但伴随着“70后”的继续成熟,将会逐渐走向深刻。

并且，由于“70后”一代的成长处于一种价值观的不稳定与动荡中，“70后”在文化上不会过于早慧，而往往显得晚熟，多从青年期的迷失与怀疑，到中年方才获得相对独立、深刻的文化理性，以及这种文化理性中的自觉意识。但是，如果我们放眼中国的百年史，那么我们会发现，正是这代人的晚熟，才使得中国在文化构建上有机会摆脱简单的“拿来主义”，才有可能构建一个全新的关于中国的现代型文化。这种由“迷失”走向“自觉”的过程，看似矛盾，却十分合理。因为，迷失的前提在于自我发现，有了自我发现才会质疑外在世界，进而寻找自我的出发点——理性。

2011年7月31日于望京

From Anomie to Rationality

–The Questioning Spirit of Seventies Generation Art

Hang Chunxiao

The concept of "Seventies generation art" arose after the year 2000 as an inclusive term for creative work by artists born during the Seventies. Academic interpretations of their works fall into two theoretical camps identified by the terms "cartoon art" and "cruel youth," which have gained some measure of acceptance. Yet present theoretical exegesis either gravitates toward pictorial symbolic features, as in the "cartoon art" thesis, or it looks at youthful impulses based on the interpretive notion of "superficial injury," as we can see in the "cruel youth" thesis. The former, being an elucidation of signs in terms of form, has difficulties grasping the spiritual quest of this generation's art. The latter builds on a contrast in life experience between the Seventies generation and their predecessors, claiming that the Seventies generation, not having gone through tumultuous social movements, lacks corresponding depth of awareness and thus characteristically shows an "impulsive" form of insight into self. This thesis seems reasonable at face value, but it assumes that a person's depth of awareness must originate from social movements , not from an ability to take stock of oneself spiritually. Thus this thesis ends up being simplistic, based on surmise and unable to touch upon the true significance of a generation's art.

Well then, being faced with the rich complexity of Seventies generation art, how should we take stock of it? Since the "Seventies generation" is a concept tied to time, our theoretical elaboration should be based on temporality. That is, its guiding thread traces a certain period's cultural issues and how these issues are visually manifested in creative work. Thus in constructing a theory of Seventies generation art, our methodology must tend toward sociological explication. We need to search for the cultural presentation and expression that time-segment's social issues. However, due to the former prevalence of pop sociology, the art field has recently shown caution in utilizing sociology, even going so far as to reject it out of hand.

Of course, as we engage in reflection on art theory, there is merit in being wary of pop sociology, with its simplistic, diagrammatic approach. But if we are thereby prompted to dismiss the connection between art and society during a specific time segment, we are doubtless headed toward the other extreme. Thus, with respect to the Seventies generation, we cannot avoid bringing society into our explications. Once we have gotten adequate understanding of their visual take on things, we should proceed to explore the psychological mechanisms behind it.

Following this line of thought, we might well ask, what are the special features of this generation's visual take on the world? The answer is that relative to the pictorial literalism and antithetical contrasts of their predecessors, works by the Seventies generation tend to stress the substance of visual language and what it itself expresses. That is, they are conversant with what is expressed by the visual material itself. In works like Yin Chaoyang's "Myth," Tu Hongtao's "Stage," and Kang Haitao's "Night-View," whether the aim of representation if individual insight or societal awareness, the materiality of language becomes a direct medium for painterly intention. Means of utilizing language, rather than pictorial signs, may become the core for a recasting of visual logic. Whether in Wang Guangle's hyper-realist terrazzo paintings or his applications of lacquer on coffin wood, abstraction for this artist is not a programmatic structure—rather, it is a spontaneous result of constant stock-taking with regard to his mode of visual presentation. Although we find distinct subject matter in works like Guan Yong's "Bookcase," Li Hui's "Two-Headed Truck," and Wang Jie's "Clothes without Wearer," nevertheless, the visual orientation, rather than being toward the subject matter, points to a mode of cognition that is inherent in the visual logic. What is more, this emphasis on language as substance, on visual logic, tends to imply an underlying "take it or leave it" kind of skeptical attitude. That is, there is no positive or negative judgment toward the object he himself depicts; instead, the object is understood as a cognitive entity presented with the aid of visual language. Being situated within his own visual logic, it furthermore becomes an object to be re-evaluated by the viewer. In one respect, their art is unlike pictures "with clear intentions" that have been influenced by political pop art. They do not like the "sloganeering" of symbolic concepts. Instead, they wish to display vision engaged in the act of taking stock. Thus even artists who draw upon cartoonish symbols, like Li Jikai, do not use cartoon images as symbols of definite concepts in their pictures; rather, they convey a "take it or leave it" visual mood that carries a sense of anomie. I should say that such visual indefiniteness and anomie evoke a stance of calling things into question. In Seventies generation art this is fairly prevalent, and it clearly sets it apart from art of the preceding period.

The questioning stance means there is no more simple affirmation or negation, and they remain wary of concrete, distinct judgments. As one of their contemporaries, I am fully in sympathy with them. Life as this generation knew it was filled with before-and-after contradictions. As is commonly known, the background they grew up in can be summed up as a "post-idealist" setting. The social ideals of the new China's early period were ruined by the Cultural Revolution. Later, the humanistic ideals of the Eighties were rendered illusory by the commercializing trends of the Nineties, as the whole society took a turn towards hard-nosed pragmatism. Growing up in this time of massive shifts, fate gave the Seventies generation the right to participate, but not the right to choose for themselves. They were put through a process of passive transformation and acclimation. They were repeatedly forced to make adjustments, changing their original world view to fit their new state of existence. In their case, there was no consistent thread in their social setting or in their way of understanding the world. Through a process of constant adjustments they came to question history and the status quo. They would not lightly oppose anything, and they habitually questioned everything in language tinged with anomie. Through such a process they arrived at rational reflection.

If we can say that Twentieth Century China was engaged in a constant process of cultural grafting, habitually learning from the West on all levels from the material to the spiritual, then we can also say that a subtle change occurred in this process when it came to the Seventies generation. The unique circumstances of this generation instilled in them an innate skeptical stance which would not let them lightly believe the "other"; they could no longer simply accept any form of thinking that did not belong to them. Through the, China has gained a chance to take stock of its own culture, to make its own choices and restructure its culture if need be. However, this process is still in an inconclusive developmental phase. Yet as the Seventies generation continues to mature, this process will gradually go deeper.

What is more, because this generation's growth took place when values were in a state of upheaval, they were not overly precocious in cultural matters; instead they showed themselves to be somewhat slow to mature. Many of them lost direction in youth and went through a skeptical phase. Only in middle age did they attain to a relatively independent, deeply rooted rationality in cultural matters, and this cultural rationality brought self-awareness. Yet if we survey China's history over the past century we will find that it has only been through the late blooming of this generation that China has gotten a chance, with respect of its cultural configuration, to break away from simple acquisitiveness. Only in this way is it possible to configure a modern culture that addresses what China really is. This process of losing direction and then moving towards self-awareness appears to be contradictory, but in truth it is quite reasonable. This is because getting lost is a pre-condition for self-discovery. Only with self-discovery can the external world be called into question, and from there one proceeds to seek the point of departure for the self—which is rationality.

July 31, 2011, Wangjing

图书在版编目(CIP)数据

重新定义:“70后”艺术中的质疑精神/杭春晓主编. -- 天津:天津人民美术出版社, 2012.2
ISBN 978-7-5305-4713-7

Ⅰ. ①重… Ⅱ. ①杭… Ⅲ. ①品鉴-中国 Ⅳ. ① J052

中国版本图书馆 CIP 数据核字(2012)第 018136 号

重新定义——“70后”艺术中的质疑精神

出 版 人:李毅峰
主　　编:杭春晓
副 主 编:魏祥奇
翻　　译:梅丹理
责任编辑:扈建立
技术编辑:郑福生
出 品 人:北京如果文化艺术发展有限公司
出版发行:天津人民美术出版社
社　　址:天津市和平区马场道 150 号
邮　　编:300050
电　　话:(022) 23283867
经　　销:全国新华书店经销
网　　址:http://www.tjrm.cn
印　　刷:北京今日新雅彩印制版技术有限公司
版　　次:2012 年 2 月第 1 版
印　　次:2012 年 2 月第 1 次印刷
开　　本:787 毫米 ×1092 毫米 1 / 8 开
印　　张:23.5
定　　价:128.00 元